Health, Housing and Social Policy:
Homes for Wealth or Health?

Lorna Arblaster and
Murray Hawtin

Published by the Socialist Health
Association

Authors' Acknowledgements

The authors would like to thank the following for their advice and support in the preparation of this report: David Adshead, Jean Conway, Roger Harris, Anne Hawtin, Christine Hogg, Geraint Hughes, Tony Jewell, Sheila McKechnie, Joy Mostyn, Janie Percy-Smith, David Pickersgill and Rosemary Ross.

Publishers' Acknowlegments

The research, printing and publication costs for this report have been generously supported by the Webb Memorial Trust.

Health, Housing and Social Policy: Homes for Wealth or Health by Lorna Arblaster and Murray Hawtin
First published by Socialist Health Association
16 Charles Square, London N1 6HP

ISBN 0 900687 21 5

Designed and printed by RAP Limited
201 Spotland Road, Rochdale, Lancs OL12 7AF

Contents

Introduction

Health, housing and social policy

Living in poor housing or being homeless are not just housing problems. They have profound implications for the health of people and of society.

In this review we first look at the association between housing, life expectancy and ill health, at the health of homeless people, at housing and health policy, and then at housing and community care. In Section Two we look at the housing policies of successive Conservative governments — policies based on reduced investment and privatisation, resulting in the shortage of decent affordable housing, homelessness and deterioration of housing stock. We then consider health and access to social housing, accountability and control in housing, and the costs of housing. The final Section outlines a more equitable housing system.

The Housing Crisis

Housing in the UK is in crisis. The central issue is the lack of affordable rented housing. This shortage is crucial since the number of households in the UK has increased from 19.4 million in 1981 to 21.8 million in 1991.[1]

Features of the housing crisis

- the number of homeless households, accepted by local authorities in England, increased from 57,200 in 1979 to 148,250 in 1992;[2]
- in London in 1992 there were 43,000 homeless households in temporary accommodation but only 17,649 vacancies in council housing;[3]
- there have been large rent increases across all the rented housing sectors, public sector (up 39%), housing associations (up 56%) and private sector renting (up 70%) in the period 1982 to 1989;[4]
- it is estimated that 62% of all tenants, in both the public and private rented sector, will receive housing benefit in 1993/94;[5]
- 68,540 houses were repossessed by building societies in 1992 because of mortgage arrears;[6]
- there were 352,050 households with mortgage arrears of at least six months in 1992;[7]
- one million home-owners have a mortgage worth more than their houses (negative equity);[8]
- social housing completions (local authority and housing associations) in 1992 reached a post-war low of 28,878, (down from 170,188 in 1977 and 107,771 in 1979);[9]
- 7,000 building firms became insolvent in 1991;[10]
- the equivalent of 600 jobs were lost in the building industry every working day in 1991 and 1992.[11] 30,000 more jobs are expected to be lost over the next two years;[12]
- over 1.4 million houses in England and Wales, are unfit for human habitation;[13]
- local authorities are effectively prevented from using the £5 billion,[14] which they hold from the sale of council houses, to build or repair property.

Poverty and housing

Poverty is closely associated with poor housing, homelessness and ill health. One commonly accepted definition of poverty is anyone with an income on or below 50% of the average income, after deduction of housing costs. On this basis in 1990/91:

- 13.5 million people (24% of the population) were living in poverty — an increase from 5 million (9% of the population) in 1979.
- 3.9 million children (31% of all children) were living in poverty — an increase from 1.4 million (10% of all children) in 1979.[15]

The effect of poverty on housing is considered in Section Two. The implications for health of widening inequalities of income are described in **Income and Health**, another publication in this series.[16]

Housing: the public costs

The idea that there is a subsidised public housing sector and an unsubsidised private sector is untrue. State subsidised home ownership has become the dominant form of public support for housing in the UK.

Government expenditure on housing fell from £13 billion in 1979/80 to £5.8 billion in 1991/92 (real terms).

Meanwhile the cost of mortgage income tax relief increased from £3.3 billion in 1979 to £6.1 billion in 1992 (£8 billion in 1990-91), (1991-92 prices). Of this, £795 million is tax relief to people earning over £35,000 a year.[17]

This 'subsidy' to home owners can be compared with the estimated £2 billion per year (additional to the £4 billion[18] already spent each year on public sector housing) which would be required to produce the 100,000 decent affordable social houses needed annually to meet the needs of homeless households over the next decade.[19]

By reducing controls and subsidies on rents the Government has shifted the burden of help with housing costs to the benefit system. In 1985/6 the cost of housing benefit was £3.1 billion (exceeding public expenditure on housing, which was then £2.8 billion). By 1992/3 housing benefit cost £7.3 billion and was paid out to 4.3 million tenants. The rise in public and private sector rents, as well as increased unemployment, are the reasons for this increase.

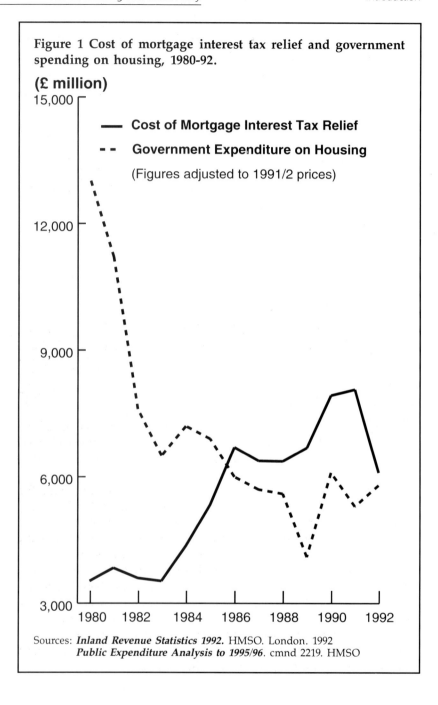

Figure 1 Cost of mortgage interest tax relief and government spending on housing, 1980-92.

(£ million)

Sources: *Inland Revenue Statistics 1992.* HMSO. London. 1992
Public Expenditure Analysis to 1995/96. cmnd 2219. HMSO

Government changes to local authority housing finances[20] mean that in future better off council tenants may find themselves paying the rebates of their poorer neighbours while the Exchequer pays out nothing at all.[21]

A fairer housing system

For a fairer housing system it is essential that there is increased government investment in housing. However, by itself this is not enough. The system of indiscriminate subsidy to owner occupiers must be reformed and people on low incomes must be enabled to meet their housing costs.

A more equitable housing policy should:

- provide sufficient social housing;
- provide social housing of a decent quality;
- promote real choice of housing tenure;
- promote local democracy in a comprehensive housing service;
- address inequalities relating to housing.

A more equitable housing system can only be achieved if the fundamental right to good quality housing for all is recognised.

The importance of housing for health and the increasing lack of affordable decent housing puts housing firmly back on the public health agenda. It is time for Government and politicians to reverse current trends and act decisively to *'pursue policies to promote choice and quality in housing, having regard to health and other benefits'* (The Health of the Nation).[22]

1 Health and housing

This Section looks at the strong association between housing tenure, including homelessness, and premature death; it then considers aspects of housing which affect health.

To most people the relationship between ill health and poor housing is self-evident. Studies on an area by area basis in towns do show an association between health and housing.[1] However the medical model of research into the effects of housing on health, which emphasises individual diagnosis and treatment, has been criticised by Hunt, who proposes a holistic approach.[2]

Researchers have found it difficult to separate the effects of housing on health from other factors such as poverty, unemployment, and social class. Nevertheless, lack of firm research evidence must not be allowed to divert attention from the underlying issues such as a serious shortage of affordable housing or be used by policy makers as an excuse for inaction.

Life expectancy

There is an association between premature death and the type of housing a person lives in. People who live in houses they own tend to live longer than those who rent their homes. Of those who rent their homes, people who rent from private landlords live longer than those who rent from the local authorities.[3] (Table I).

Table I Mortality (SMR)[1] by Housing Tenure and Social Class (males 15-64 years, 1970-75)			
Social Class	Housing tenure		
	Owner occupied	Privately rented	Local authority tenancy
I	79	93	99
II	74	104	99
III Non-manual	79	112	121
III Manual	83	99	104
IV	83	100	106
V	98	126	123

Source: Medical Statistics Division, OPCS, quoted by Townsend and Davidson in **Inequalities in Health**, 1992.

1. The standardised mortality ratio, SMR, is used to compare death rates between different groups. It is a measure of the actual deaths in any year given as a percentage of expected deaths. The lower the number the longer people live.

Death rates are also related to where people live. Men who were owner occupiers in residential retirement areas have been found to live longer than owner occupiers in inner-city areas.[4] (Table II) Men who rented low quality inner city accommodation died earlier than other groups, but those who rented privately in inner city areas died at a slightly earlier age than those living in the same area but who rented from the local authority. These findings reflect income levels, employment, health including mental health, age, and ethnicity.

Table II   Deaths in 1971 — 1981 of men in different residential areas by housing tenure (1971)

Housing area	Housing Tenure		
	Owner occupied SMR	Privately rented SMR	Local Authority SMR
Residential retirement areas	83	97	104
New towns	78	78	112
Older industrial settlements with low stress	94	115	119
Inner city areas with low-quality, older housing	112	137	134

Source: Fox, Jones and Goldblatt, 1984.

For both men and women, owner occupiers lived longer and people in local authority housing died earlier than the average.[5] (Table III)

Table III Mortality of men and women in 1971-81 by housing tenure (England and Wales)

Housing Tenure	Standardised Mortality Ratios	
	Men (aged 15-64 years at death)	Women (aged 15-59 years at death)
Owner-occupied	84	83
Privately rented	109	106
Local authority	115	117

Source: Goldblatt, OPCS LS, 1990.

Deaths of children

A study of deaths of children in 1971 showed that there was a significant association between the deaths, particularly of young children, and the extent of overcrowding, lack of basic amenities, male unemployment and living in a council house.[6] In another study stillbirth rates and infant death rates were higher among babies born to private tenants compared with those born to owner occupiers.[7]

Houses in multiple occupation

Bedsits and shared houses are described as houses in multiple occupation (HMOs). They are home to two and a half million people (5% of the population). Home Office statistics show that residents of HMOs are ten times more likely to die in a fire than residents of other dwellings.[8] Makeshift cooking arrangements, dangerous heating appliances and inadequate means of escape are often the cause. One study found that there was no satisfactory means of escape in 56% of bed and breakfast hostels despite the fact that 80% of the properties had been issued with a fire certificate.[9]

Homeless rough sleepers and hostel dwellers

'Crisis', a charity for the homeless, identified 86 homeless people who died in London in the year to August 1991.[10] Most were men (82%), and their average age was 47 years. (The average life expectancy for men in the UK is 73 years, and, for women 79 years.) Nearly a quarter died by suicide, and Crisis considered that two thirds of all the deaths were preventable. They estimate that homeless people are 150 times more likely to be fatally assaulted, 34 times more likely to commit suicide, 8 times more likely to die in an accident and 3 times more likely to die of pneumonia and hypothermia than the average person. The Government claims to be interested in preventing deaths, including deaths from suicide among severely mentally ill people, and has set targets to reduce these in The Health of the Nation.

However, replying to a parliamentary question about the number of people found dead on the streets in London in the last five years, Mr Baldry, Secretary of State for the Environment, said *'this information is not held centrally'*.[11] Increasingly, parliamentary replies to questions about housing issues take this form. By not collecting data the Government can avoid responsibility.

Fatal accidents at home[12]

In 1991 there were over 5,000 fatal accidents in the home in the UK. This represents 40% of all fatal accidents. In comparison, in the 1980s an average of 6,000 people were killed each year on the road.

Home-related accidents are the cause of a quarter of all deaths of children aged between 10 and 14 years of age, and are the commonest cause of death in children aged over 1 year.

Analysis of Home Accident Surveillance System (HASS) data showed that almost half of all accidents to children were associated with architectural features in and around the home.[13]

There is a close correlation between home accidents and socio-economic factors such as income and class, revealing that poorer people have more accidents. The sale of council houses, and the reduction in house building and repair, have resulted in thousands of families from low socio-economic groups being confined to unsafe and otherwise unhealthy housing.

The main causes of home accidents are falls (60%) and fires (15%). Falls account for 82% of all fatal accidents in the home to people over age 75. Stairs and uneven slippery floors are frequently the cause. House fires result in approximately 700 deaths a year. The incidence of domestic fires is associated with unemployment, low socio-economic status, and with living in rented property.[14] In 1987, 18% of people who died in fires were aged 60-74, and a quarter were over 75 years.

Carbon monoxide poisoning causes about 100 deaths a year, often because of carbon monoxide fumes from badly installed or maintained gas appliances.

Cold

On average there were 168 deaths from hypothermia during each March quarter for the years 1979 to 1990 (range 74 to 294). About 40,000 more people die in Britain in winter time than in the summer, especially the old and the very young. When the winter is very cold there are about 8,000 extra deaths for each degree Celsius the temperature falls lower than average. These deaths are usually recorded as due to chest disease, heart disease or stroke. A survey of old people found that 25% worried about the cost of heating their homes and that this deterred them from using as much heat as they would like.[15] In a mild winter between mid-November and mid-December one survey found that 96% of over 65 year olds lived in living rooms at a temperature below the recommended 21.1°C; 84% were below the 1961 recommended level of 18.3°C, and 64% were less than 16°C.

Efficient heating and insulation are important factors in cold related deaths. There are fewer excess winter deaths in European countries with colder climates but warmer homes. During the 1960s and 1970s the UK had the highest winter mortality ratio for temperate and cold countries in North America and Europe. The use of central heating in Britain increased from 13% in 1964 to 66% by 1984. This led to a decline in excess winter mortality.[16]

In the UK in 1991 some 6.6 million households suffered fuel poverty because of the energy inefficiency of their homes. To bring their homes up to the standard needed to provide affordable warmth would cost £2,500 per house, a total of £16.5 billion.[17]

Illness and housing

Reports in several recent publications show that badly designed and poorly built houses with inadequate heating, dampness, lack of space, poor lighting, and shared amenities, contribute to poor health.[18 19 20 21 22 23]

The Health and Lifestyle Survey looked at the health of people in different housing tenures (Table IV).[24] Overall, owner occupiers were in better health than council tenants. The difference was particularly marked between non-manual women in owner occupied housing and non-manual women in rented accommodation who were in much poorer health.

The National Child Development Survey has been studying 17,000 people born in 1958. There were marked differences between young people in owner-occupied and local authority accommodation at ages 7 and 23 for five different health measures (height, 'malaise', self-reported health, hospital admissions and psychiatric morbidity).[25] The health of council tenants was found to be poorer than that of owner occupiers. These differences were especially marked among young women.

A study in Gateshead in 1983 found that people living in 'bad' areas of council estates reported poorer health, more chronic illness, more recent illness, and more symptoms of depression than those in 'good' areas. One third reported housing defects which they considered affected their health.

Table IV Proportions of people by housing tenure in selected combined health categories.

Health Category	Owner-occupier		Council tenant		Other	
	Non-manual	Manual	Non-manual	Manual	Non-manual	Manual
MEN						
Good/excellent	39	35	31	28	35	32
Poor/very poor	17	20	25	29	16	27
Good health but poor psycho-social health	10	9	10	6	7	10
Number of men, N (N=100)	1,096	1,084	165	758	74	98
WOMEN						
Good/excellent	40	31	20	20	30	31
Poor/very poor	22	23	36	30	21	22
Good health but poor psycho-social health	17	18	16	22	21	23
Number of women, N. (N=100)	1,305	1,186	282	938	105	112

Source: Blaxter M. **Health and Lifestyles.** Tavistock/Routledge London. 1990.

It has been found that cancer is more common among council tenants than owner occupiers, and that council tenants have a poorer survival rate than owner occupiers irrespective of age, cause of death and prognosis of the cancer.[26] Council tenants are more likely to go to the doctor at a later stage of the cancer development than owner occupiers and this delay is likely to be a cause of the survival differences.

The distribution of high levels of overcrowding in the past in north-west Wales was consistent with areas of unexplained high death rates from stomach cancer.[27] Besides lack of adequate food storage, overcrowding in the home during childhood could be a major determinant of stomach cancer. By encouraging the spread of infection this could influence the risk of cancer.

Respiratory illness and housing

People who live in areas of poor housing in Gateshead reported more respiratory symptoms than those living in 'good areas'. These health problems are largely associated with flats rather than houses, and with older accommodation. Although houses are the most healthy form of dwelling, this is not so for the 'inter war' housing estates where people have a high rate of respiratory symptoms.[28]

The house dust mite and fungal spores both thrive in damp housing conditions. The debris of the house dust mite, particularly its faecal pellets, acts as an allergen and can cause chest problems such as wheezing.

Condensation, which is almost pure water, unlike penetrating or rising damp where the water contains salts, encourages the growth of fungal spores. These can also cause allergies such as asthma, a runny nose (rhinitis), and inflammation of the lung (alveolitis).

The English House Condition Survey 1991, found that dampness was present in 10% of occupied public sector and 24% of occupied private sector dwellings. However others have estimated that between 25% and 33% of homes in Britain are, to some extent, affected by damp. In one study, owner-occupied homes were less damp than rented homes (8% compared with 30%) and had less mould growth (5% compared to 19%). This difference accounted for the differences in wheezing by housing tenure. Among homes unaffected by damp or mould, wheezing was similar in people in the rented sector (11.1%) and in the owner occupied homes (10.6%). In Edinburgh the incidence of wheeze and chesty cough amongst children sleeping in damp bedrooms was twice (22%) that of those who slept in dry rooms (11%).[29] Children living in damp houses, especially where fungal mould was present, had higher rates of respiratory symptoms, which were unrelated to smoking in the household. They also had higher rates of infection and stress.[30]

> In 1990 a boy of 5 years was awarded £12,000 compensation for aggravation of his asthma caused by living in a damp council flat in Peckham, South London.

Tuberculosis infection has traditionally been associated with low socio-economic status and poor housing. Poor housing was a feature of an outbreak in Leeds in which 21 people were infected, 18 of them children.[31]

Mental health and housing

Various aspects of housing can be a source of mental distress such as living alone, living in overcrowded accommodation or in unsatisfactory environments. Vandalism, powerlessness in the face of increasing levels of crime, poor security, harassment — racial, sexual and physical — increase stress. High levels of boarded up properties and turnover rates of occupancy can add to this distress.

The poorly designed and untested building systems used to construct high-rise and deck access flats in the 1960s have resulted in many people now having to live in cold, damp, noisy, and potentially dangerous property, often surrounded by rubbish and graffiti. Some tenants still live in fear of another partial collapse such as that which killed five people in Ronan Point in 1968. Much of this housing is unsuitable for families, with little space for normal play, considerable social isolation, poor control over public stairwells and entrances, and constant fear of vandalism and crime — all factors which increase mental distress.

People living in poor quality flats have been found to have more mental symptoms than those in houses, an effect which increases with the number of floors.[32] The presence of mould is associated with depression.

In January 1989 in Southwell, London, a middle aged couple in a high rise block died after petrol was poured through their letter box and set alight. They could not be rescued because they had barricaded themselves behind a steel grille fearing that the flat would be broken into. Later, a £3 million refurbishment with electronic surveillance, reinforced doors for each maisonette and a concierge system, was carried out. This reduced the burglaries from two a week to a rare event, and resulted in improved morale of the residents.[33]

High levels of mental ill health have been found in inner city areas, in poor council estates as well as in high rise flats. In the Divis flats in Belfast 70% of households included someone who was depressed, or who showed other signs of mental stress. There, a military presence, violence, poor housing, poverty and unemployment all contribute to mental distress. The absence of shops, schools and play areas has been particularly identified as a major contribution to problems in new housing estates. For women, the stresses of living in houses in a bad state of repair, with poor access to services and employment, are made worse by a housing system which fails to recognise women's needs.[34]

A study in Newcastle-upon-Tyne has shown stress to be strongly related to wanting to move house, a burglary in the last year, or the existence of damp which the respondent considered to affect their health. (see page 50) Long standing disability in a 'nice' area gave a stress rating of 24 compared with a rating of 40 in a 'terrible' area. Higher stress levels were associated with frequent contact with the health services.

Other housing factors which are a source of stress are structural defects causing cold and damp houses, noise, insulation and ventilation problems, delays in getting good quality repairs done, infestations, cooking smells and the presence of asbestos.

Overcrowding is believed by many to be associated with mental distress.[35][36] Women in crowded households may have difficulty controlling the amount of social interaction they have with other members of the household. Often they do not have the privacy needed for health, and there is no clear separation between domestic responsibilities and leisure. Women at home with small children in poor overcrowded conditions are particularly likely to be depressed.[37]

Fear of eviction may lead to clinical depression, particularly in women, and stress is often associated with powerlessness in people seeking suitable accommodation. For many, without money to buy a home, the possibility of being rehoused is remote. This is particularly true for physically and mentally disabled people, for single people and for couples without children.

Household features affecting health

Water

Water prices have increased almost 50% in the past five years. The water industry declared a pre-tax profit in excess of £1.5 billion in 1992. In the same year 21,000 households were disconnected from their water supply.

19

Table V Water Disconnections	
1990/91	7,600
1991/92	21,300
1992/93	18,600

Disconnection rates vary between regions, and this is thought to be due to differences in commercial practice. Southern Water has a disconnection rate of 23 per 10,000 billings (average 4.2 per 10,000). Unlike gas and electricity there is no code of practice about when disconnection is or is not appropriate. Many local councils are calling for a ban on water disconnections.[38] In Scotland water disconnection is not allowed and debt collection takes place through the courts.

Disconnections can lead to a total breakdown in hygiene, which is essential to prevent diseases such as dysentery.

Rising incidence of dysentery and hepatitis A

- Confirmed cases of dysentery in England and Wales were 2,011 and 1,489 in 1989 and 1990, and rose to 8,071 in 1991 where the disease was presumed to be contracted in Great Britain.[39] This was the highest number for almost 20 years.
- The total cost of dysentery to the public sector in 1991 in England and Wales was estimated as £1,175,288.[40]
- Notified cases of hepatitis A increased from 1,126 in 1987 to 3,431 in 1989 and 5,610 in 1991.[41] Community outbreaks have occurred among people in poor housing and in areas with high rates of water disconnection.

Access to washing facilities is an important factor in determining health. A national survey of temporary accommodation in 1987 found that on average 16 people were sharing a bath and 20 were sharing a WC. Studies of people rehoused from slums have shown that standards of hygiene rise when clean water is freely available, even without specific educational programmes.

Water metering, which results in higher costs for water, is a particular problem for families with young children or people who, because of conditions such as colitis, have extra water requirements.

Noise

Other people's noise can be a source of great stress. Complaints to local authorities have risen 20-fold in the last 20 years, and in one study 56% of people said they had been annoyed by noise at home. It is a particular problem of system built houses, in areas with poor housing management, and where there is a mix of young and old people.

More than half of the walls of newly completed houses failed to meet the Building Research Establishment's recommended standards in respect of noise transmission between buildings. A third of the floors were very poor for the insulation of sound.

Noise is now a statutory nuisance and local authorities have to investigate reasonable complaints. In July 1993 a Leicester woman was fined £12,500 for refusing to turn down a radio. Bristol's Noise Mediation Scheme is exploring different ways of resolving complaints about noise.[42]

Chemicals in the home

Radon is a gas which may be present in houses and which emits high energy alpha particles. It is the single largest source of exposure to radiation for most people in the UK. In Britain, up to 12% of cases of myeloid leukaemia may be caused by radon.[43] However the study failed to link exposure to radon with the development of lung cancer. This is interesting since exposure to radon in uranium miners has been found to cause lung cancer.

The National Radiological Protection Board advise that the average domestic exposure to radon of a concentration of 20 Bq/m^3 carries an estimated lifetime risk of developing lung cancer of 0.3%. This means that one in 20 cases of lung cancer in Britain may be caused by domestic exposure to radon.[44]

Radon enters the home mainly through soil gas. The levels vary throughout the country. Houses in Devon and Cornwall are particularly affected. Houses can be modified to reduce the level of radon.[45]

Asbestos has been used for insulation, for lagging pipes, and to reinforce building materials. Where asbestos is intact there is little risk, but with deterioration there is a risk to health. The risk varies according to the type of fibre, blue asbestos being more dangerous than white. The removal of asbestos releases fibres, which are a health risk. Professional removal is very expensive and problematic for tenants and local authorities.

Nitrogen dioxide which comes from gas cookers is associated with reports of respiratory illness in children.[46]

Formaldehyde has many uses including foam insulation, synthetic carpets and pressed wood products. It can cause irritation of the mucous membranes and other symptoms.

Pests

Cockroaches like warm wet conditions. System built properties of the 1960s, such as the Divis flats in Belfast, a third of the tower blocks in Hackney and the Moss Side Centre in Manchester, are especially prone to infestation. In the Moss Side Centre immense populations of cockroaches built up in the multi-service ducts which gave access to the kitchens and bathrooms of 200 maisonettes. The risk to tenants is from:

- germs transferred from house to house;
- cockroach allergy (symptoms vary from those similar to mild hay-fever to severe shock) caused by the bodies of dead cockroaches remaining in the ducting;
- from the use of pesticides to kill the cockroaches;
- from stress and the personal inconvenience of the infestation.

Poor maintenance of sewers, increased demolition work, food waste and tipping are some of the causes for an increase in the number of **rats** seen above ground in London and other places.[47] Poor facilities for, and bad practice in, waste food disposal are major causes of rat infestation in buildings. Because they often live in drains their bodies are a source of food poisoning and other disease-causing organisms. They also transmit leptospirosis through contact with their urine.

Accidental injury

Of the 3 million non-fatal domestic accidents each year 2.2 million people are treated in hospital and another 900,000 are treated by their general practitioners. More than 300,000 of these are people aged 65 and over who require hospital attention. The cost of domestic accidents to the health service in England and Wales is about £300 million a year.

Each year there are approximately 750,000 accidents to children under 16 years of age in the home. Of these about 5,000 children are permanently disabled.

Childhood accidents show a definite variation according to social class.[48] During a one year period in Haringey, London, almost 20% of children under five attended an accident and emergency department, three quarters of them because of an accident at home. Children from the most deprived parts of the borough were four times as likely to have an accident as those from the most affluent parts. There was a significant correlation between accident rates and unemployment, overcrowding, rented tenure, poor education of the parents and low social class.

'Deprived children' from a one-parent family or from a very large family, living in poor housing conditions or on low income, are at increased risk of serious accidents. By 11 years of age 'deprived' children are more likely than others to have received a burn, a scald, or serious flesh wounds in an accident at home. One in seven of the 'deprived' children had suffered a burn or scald compared with one in eleven of the other children; four times more had received a flesh wound requiring ten or more stitches.

There are currently no statistics of the number of accidents to children living in temporary accommodation, but there is concern that such children may be at high risk of accidental injury because of their accommodation. The Child Accident Prevention Trust (CAPT 1991) found that most of the temporary accommodation allocated by local authorities and others to homeless families with children is ill designed, ill equipped and ill maintained. For 72% of families in bed and breakfast in London there was no safe place for the children to play. HASS estimate that it would add 5% to the cost of a house to incorporate the safety features identified in research by the Child Accident Prevention Trust.

In 1988 in the UK 27,000 accidents were attributable to non-safety glass in doors and windows of which nearly half were associated with glass in doors. Over a third (40%) involve children under 15 years of age. Lowry considers that the regulations and terminology relating to domestic glass are inadequate and confusing.[49] In her opinion all architectural glass used in new houses should be toughened glass meeting British Standard 6202.

Homelessness and health

Temporary, bed and breakfast type, accommodation

The poor health of homeless families in temporary accommodation is well documented.[50] [51] In North West Thames the health of adults living in temporary accommodation was compared with that of other regional residents.[52] The incidence of long term illness or disability among the homeless was two and a half times that of other residents of the same age. Mental distress and ill health was twice as great in the homeless group (45%), compared with local residents (20%).

Mental health problems such as depression, relationship problems, isolation, suicide attempts, and heavy drinking are higher among homeless people in temporary accommodation. Emotional and behaviourial problems of children in temporary accommodation are a cause for concern, particularly developmental delay, aggression, poor sleep and bed wetting.

Women who become homeless during pregnancy are three times as likely to be admitted to hospital during the pregnancy and are more likely to have anaemia or a Caesarian section than women who become homeless after the birth. Homeless women are more likely than other women to have a small premature baby, which has difficulty in breathing.[53] For people in temporary accommodation infectious diseases — such as chest infections, diarrhoea and vomiting, dysentery, measles, mumps, chicken pox and hepatitis — are an additional problem.

Becoming homeless is extremely socially disrupting. The usual social support network is lost. Parents are unable to provide what they know to be necessary for their children's development and welfare. It is made worse by not knowing how long the family will remain in temporary accommodation.

Rough sleepers and hostel dwellers

A third of homeless rough sleepers and hostel dwellers abuse alcohol.[54] It was the reason for 70% of 2,349 consultations by men at a clinic for homeless people and for 6.5% of those by women. Health problems of alcohol abuse include duodenal ulcers, malnutrition, peripheral neuritis, weak legs, blackouts and injuries. Aggressive behaviour can give rise to isolation and guilt, but can also lead to arrest, loss of employment and barring from health or hostel provision, and from access to GPs and health care services.

Drug abuse has been found to be below 10% in this group,[55] and only 3% experienced accommodation problems because of this.

Half of these homeless people have chronic physical illnesses,[56] and a fifth have more than one disease. Musculoskeletal, respiratory and skin disorders[57] are common problems. Other conditions are gastrointestinal problems, including ulcers, and tuberculosis.[58] In the USA there has been an increase in TB cases caused by resistant organisms.

Levels of deviant behaviour and detachment from society are high. In one study of 48 hostel dwellers in Oxford measures of socially unacceptable behaviour, such as violence and sexual offensiveness, showed that almost half were as severely disabled as the most disabled long stay patients in hospitals.[59] Psychiatrically untrained workers and volunteers who staffed two hostels for the homeless were, in effect, looking after the equivalent of patients from two long stay psychiatric wards. They were also caring for a further 98 homeless residents.

Severe mental illness affects about a third of this group. Crisis at Christmas found that 41% gave a history of severe mental illness, and 22% were affected at the time of interview.[60] For comparison such conditions exist in about 1% of adults in the general population. Another study of men in a hostel found that 31% were diagnosed as schizophrenic. Two thirds of these were not in contact with the psychiatric services.[61] Of 122 homeless men, 12 were actively depressed, 10 were manic-depressives. Several had suicidal thoughts and 17 (14%) had attempted suicide in the past, some of them very recently. Of 43 women referred to a visiting psychiatrist at a hostel for single homeless women in London, 80% were mentally ill and 21% were schizophrenic.[62] Alcohol problems associated with mental illness have been found in 38% of men and 32% of women.[63]

Young homeless

The number of single homeless people under the age of 30 is increasing because of unemployment and the withdrawal in 1988 of income support from most unemployed 16 and 17 year olds.[64] Among those using a young people's shelter 41% had grown up in care. In 1990, 1,426 young people were prosecuted for begging and sleeping rough.

Young people under 25 years old are often seen as a separate group. However their problems are similar to those of older homeless rough sleepers and hostel dwellers.[65] These include being penniless, malnutrition, alcohol and substance abuse, sexual abuse, as well as fear of AIDS/HIV and pregnancy.

Staff of a voluntary organisation (Doorstep) in Grimsby were concerned that many young people did not have enough money to buy food, and may not have eaten for several days. They also reported that

30% of their clients were unable to read. Most needed supportive training in how to look after themselves.

Often when accommodation has been found for young people, other problems then surface. Low self-esteem is widespread. Often caused by rejection, it is sometimes associated with physical and sexual abuse (in some studies 40% have been sexually abused). Most hostel staff do not have the training to help young people work through such experiences. The risks from prostitution (both male and female), exploitation associated with drugs, HIV, sexually transmitted diseases and pregnancy are high for homeless young people.

Mentally vulnerable people

Homeless mentally vulnerable people who commit crimes may not be diverted from the criminal system although in some cases their offences are relatively minor.

Nearly two thirds of 334 men remanded to Winchester prison for psychiatric reports between 1979 and 1983 were homeless on arrest.[66] A third were charged with burglary and theft, of which many were *'minor incidents involving hungry and destitute men, such as shoplifting food, stealing pies and bottles of milk from private houses. 28 men had been charged with fraud and deception, often concerning failure to pay for a meal'.*

By finding their way into prison many mentally vulnerable people obtain the only care and treatment that anyone is prepared to offer them.

Access to health care

Many single homeless people do not register with GPs and use accident and emergency departments for primary care.

In the North West Thames Region homeless people in temporary accommodation use the health services more than other residents.[67] However, this use was less than their health profile might suggest. General practitioner consultations by the homeless were almost twice (29%) that of local residents (16%).

Homeless people are more likely to live some distance from the surgery; 18% lived 8 km or more from the surgery compared with 3% of local residents.

Other findings of the survey show that visits to casualty departments in the previous 14 days were much higher by the homeless (13%) than by local residents (3%). Being a hospital inpatient (excluding obstetrics) in the previous 12 months was more common for the homeless (13%), than for local residents (10%). However another study[68] found that admission to hospital was 4.5 times more common in this group. In Southampton some families found it necessary to be registered with three different practices in the course of a year. Health visitor and midwifery service managers reported the difficulty of monitoring continuity of care for families who were subject to frequent moves because of the local authority's housing policies.[69]

In West Lambeth people of no fixed abode, sleeping rough or in hostels, were almost five times as likely to require hospital admission as the general population. In Bloomsbury they accounted for 8.7% of all hospital admissions.

A study of GP surgeries in Aberdeen found that the location of the surgeries favoured the established middle class districts of the city, and that deprived areas were poorly served. High levels of car ownership in the owner occupied outlying areas of the city extended accessibility to services quite markedly, while there continued to be very low levels of accessibility in the outlying local authority estates.

Community care and housing

The Conservatives have applied the philosophy of the market to social services. They have reduced the provider role of local authority social services departments (SSDs) and expanded the role of purchasing care. SSDs have to assess the care needs of certain groups. These include the elderly, those with learning difficulties, the long term sick, the physically disabled, women who have experienced domestic violence, and misusers of drugs and alcohol. And, from April 1993, 85% of the money transferred to local authorities from the DSS (£399 million in 1993, and estimated by local authorities to be £135 million short) is to be used to buy care from private and voluntary organisations.[70] Local authorities are now responsible for the assessment and financial support of people in private and voluntary homes.

The Griffiths report in 1988 played down the role of housing in community care as restricted to *'bricks and mortar with no social or inter-agency significance'.*[71] Housing departments rejected this as *'the false assumption that there is a clear dividing line between responsibility for bricks and mortar and the provision of social support. In practice the two are inextricably bound together'.*[72]

27

In response to the Griffiths report, the Major City Councils' Housing Group[73] were concerned about:

- the lack of data on vulnerable groups to begin to assess their housing needs;
- lack of national guidelines on good practice of providing for these groups;
- the need for adequate financial resources to cover the increased costs of care in the community;
- the difficulty of co-ordinating the many agencies involved.

They identified a need for:

- a national system to collect and disseminate data;
- additional resources to cover increased costs;
- better local collaboration, with equal partnership for housing, health and social services;
- a recognition of Housing's responsibilities beyond 'bricks and mortar';

In 1989 the white paper, *Caring for People,*[74] acknowledged that *'housing is a vital component of community care and often the key to independent living'*. Housing departments were concerned that with social services departments being given the lead role in the joint planning of community care they would underestimate the practicalities of providing housing: *'the fact that there is still an expectation that housing departments should be able to make public sector lettings available on request for community care clients is an unrealistic expectation nowadays. Housing authorities also feel that they are left to pick up the pieces of previous 'failed' community care policies, with lack of support from social services.'*[75] The frustrations of joint planning for community care[76] have left many housing departments feeling marginalised.

The focus on providing care services in the home has diverted attention from people without homes — for example those living with parents, in longstay hospitals, in residential homes, and the homeless; also those about to leave care, leave acute hospitals, or leave prison and who have nowhere to live. Unnecessary institutionalisation should be considered when housing assessments are being made. There is little experience of assessing the housing needs of these groups and the Government has not helped. For example the 1992 Circular on Housing and Community Care, produced by the Departments of the Environment and Health, did not offer any practical advice on how to assess housing need.

Traditionally the housing needs of a much more narrowly

defined group, those with 'special housing needs', have been provided, as Watson and Ward point out, through mini systems:[77]

- housing associations have come to bilateral agreements with statutory and voluntary agencies on particular schemes;
- health and social services have developed their own residential units;
- housing authorities have been responsible for the homeless and some 'vulnerable' people;
- private operators have set up residential homes largely funded through social security benefits covering both housing and care costs.

The housing departments' contribution to special needs housing, like that of social services and health departments, has been mainly through special schemes rather than the 'ordinary' housing concept of community care. The group home or hostel is the too familiar model to professionals. For the 'ordinary' housing concept to be promoted clients and/or agencies representing them should be consulted at an early stage in the planning process.

Investment in social housing is set to fall by £1 billion over the next two years. Housing associations, who are taking over from the local authorities in providing special housing, are funded through the Housing Corporation. There has been a decrease of 42% in funding for new special needs housing since 1989/90.

The resources for community care are inadequate, and at present most of it is used to support elderly people in residential accommodation. Research by North British Housing Association found that 58% of highly, or very highly, dependent tenants received two hours or less of home care each week. The problem of elderly people having to sell their homes to pay for residential accommodation is also becoming apparent.

A study funded by Wessex Regional Health Authority, the NHS Management Executive and local authority participants is collecting data on housing needs and supply, to produce a model for assessments.[78] It will then produce policy proposals to be agreed and implemented by the relevant funding and planning bodies (housing, social services, health commissions, and special needs housing forums).

Such a study will identify a large unmet need which, to be remedied, requires adequate funding. Besides collaboration on planning and assessments, health, housing, social services and the special needs housing forums should be united in their demands for increased investment in housing and social support.

Health promotion

The Government is not addressing the matters covered in this Section. It has identified some causes of serious illness or early death which, in its view, *'offer scope for effective action'*. These are set out in the Health of the Nation,[79] together with targets and dates by which to measure 'achievements'. However, to achieve these targets the Government aims to change the behaviour of individuals, focussing the causes of ill health on individual behaviour, such as smoking and over-eating.

The emphasis on individual behaviour obscures the impact of the environmental causes of ill health. A government concerned about the health of the people should work to improve housing and tackle poverty and unemployment. These are the real causes of inequality in health.

Conservative housing policy, by creating a shortage of affordable housing, has resulted in more families having to live in temporary accommodation (see Section 2). Such a housing environment is a potential danger to health, particularly as 72% of families in bed and breakfast in London have no safe place for their children to play,[80] putting at risk the health, and in some cases the lives, of children.

The Health of the Nation targets improvement in the health of mentally ill people. However, mental illness is often associated with living in poor housing. To help the severely mentally ill, especially to prevent suicides, those responsible for mental health should be lobbying for more and better social housing, particularly supported accommodation and care.

The collaborative working between environmental health departments and health authorities for investigating, monitoring, and bringing under control outbreaks of communicable diseases should include the monitoring of housing conditions.

Conclusion

At a basic level housing is necessary for shelter, for warmth, for sanitation and for security; and beyond this, for personal development. Without housing even basic needs cannot be met, resulting, for some people, in death on the streets before the age of fifty.

Housing which is badly designed, poorly maintained and in

some cases lacking amenities such as water, impairs health, resulting in infections, chronic disease and accidents.

Decent housing is a prerequisite for good health. Government policies which prevent the acquisition of decent housing for all are responsible for damaging the people's health.

Social housing in crisis

This Section starts by looking at the housing policies pursued by Conservative governments since 1979, based on reducing public expenditure and privatising public assets. It then examines briefly some consequences of this disastrous approach.

Government housing policy

Conservative strategy towards housing has been guided by two key principles;
- reduced public investment in social housing;
- the privatisation of local authority housing stock.

Reduced social housing investment

The determination of successive Conservative governments to cut and control capital expenditure and public borrowing has had a major impact on housing. Housing suffered the severest of all expenditure cuts falling from £13.1 billion in 1979/80 to £5.8 billion in 1991/92. Over the same period spending on social security, education, health and social services increased in real terms. (Table VI)

Table VI Government spending in real terms on various functions 1979/80 and 1991/92 (billions)[1]				
	Housing	Health	Education	Social Security
1979/80	£13.1	£25.6	£24.4	£46.6
1991/92	£ 5.8	£37.4	£29.6	£70.0

As a percentage of total expenditure, government spending on housing has also fallen since 1979. (Table VII).

Table VII Government spending as a proportion of all spending 1979/80 and 1991/92[2]					
	Housing	Defence	Health	Education	Social Security
1979/80	7.3%	12.2%	14.3%	13.6%	26.0%
1991/92	2.7%	10.5%	17.0%	13.6%	32.0%

Not only were the cuts in housing expenditure large and introduced rapidly, they were over-achieved. In 1981/2 they were found to be one and a half times larger than had been intended by the Government in 1980.[3]

This economy was targeted at local authorities. The Government's own programmes were affected less, and did not extend to the public expenditure associated with mortgage interest tax relief for home owners.

The Government has used various means to reduce expenditure on social housing. Each year local authorities submit a programme for council building, maintenance and housing developments in their area, and bid to the Department of the Environment (DoE) for borrowing permission to cover this Housing Investment Programme (HIP). In the 1980s the Government used this system to reduce local authority spending. In 1978/9 HIP borrowing allocations were £4,388 million but by 1986/87 had fallen to £1,412 million, a reduction of nearly 70%.

Many local authorities explored other sources to finance capital schemes, including the use of capital receipts from council house sales. However legislation in 1989 enabled the Government to tighten its control over local authorities so that it now allocates a 'credit approval' to them, further limiting their borrowing arrangements.

In 1989/90 councils invested £5,123 million in housing. In 1990/91 this fell by over 50% to £2,406, in 1991/92 by nearly a further 25% to £1,891 million. It was expected to fall to £1,529 in 1992/93.

This lack of investment has had devastating effects on many areas of housing, especially on the number of public sector houses which have been built — a number which had been growing for 60 years up until the 1980s, since when it has fallen every year.

Lack of investment has drastically affected the building industry where 12,000 building firms became insolvent during 1990 and 1991. By early 1993 some 450,000 building jobs had been lost. (It is estimated that a further 30,000 jobs will be lost in the two years 1994 and 1995). Each unemployed person costs the state about £8,900 per year in benefits and lost tax. In addition, in two years, the collapse of the construction industry is estimated to have cost the Exchequer £2,700 million, so that the total cost of the recession in the building industry may well have been over £4,000 million.

The privatisation of local authority housing stock

By 1990 one and a half million public sector dwellings had been sold representing the largest of the Government's privatisation programmes. Receipts for the period 1979 to 1989 were £17.58 billion (43% of all privatisation proceeds over that time),[4] and by the end of 1993 this had risen to £28 billion which is *more than the total of the next three largest privatisation — gas, electricity and BT — put together*.[5] The Government's programme was achieved by:

- providing ways for transferring council housing to other tenures;
- ensuring the unpopularity of council housing;
- taking more direct control of local authority housing.

In 1979 the Conservatives regarded their 'right to buy' policy as key to their election success. Their aim was to expand owner occupation at the expense of council housing and in this they have been remarkably successful. However by the mid 1980s, despite further discounts, sales of council properties had slowed down, so the Government sought new means of transferring property from the local authority sector. The Voluntary Transfer Scheme allowed councils to sell off whole estates; the 'Tenants' Choice' with its rigged ballot system gave alternative landlords the opportunity to buy estates; and Housing Action Trusts were designed to remove estates from council control, initially in favour of an undemocratic trust, and later to be sold off privately.

The latest attempt to encourage council tenants to buy their homes is a 'Rents into Mortgage' scheme, which is on trial in Scotland and, which will shortly be introduced into England. Progress in experimental areas has been slow, and the average cost of administration is nearly £3,000 per sale.

How has such an integral component of our welfare system as housing been so systematically dismantled with so little public outcry? The answer is complex involving large vested interests in private property, the facade of a safety-net for the very worst off, the low profile of housing issues by all political parties, and the proven phenomenon that owner occupiers are more likely to vote Conservative. Council housing was seen by the Conservatives in the 1970s as a strong base of Socialism, and because of this the Conservatives were determined to reduce the public housing sector to a minimum.

When in power the Conservatives set about systematically to undermine many of the functions of local authorities, thereby effectively discrediting them as inefficient, profligate, or too politically motivated.

> *'We'll be acting to end — once and for all — the monopoly power of arrogant Labour councils over the management of housing estates.'*
>
> John Major February 1992

A massive increase in the housing stock in the 1960s and 1970s made many housing departments centrally based, inflexible and unwieldy and so there was some justification of the criticisms of the local authorities. The badly designed and badly built estates added to the enormous physical and social problems facing managers. Despite these factors having been aggravated by decreased investment, housing authorities' performance has been improving over the last decade.

The Government has reduced local authorities' power over housing services in several ways: it controls the reduced capital borrowing powers of councils, attempts to impose unaccountable Housing Action Trusts on estates, gives landlords the right to attempt to buy estates (so called 'tenants choice'); and the DOE controls the designation of Renewal Areas and Estate Action spending.

The effects of the privatisation programme has been far reaching, advancing greatly the long-term trend of tenure restructuring shown in figure 2.

Owner occupation increased from 58% of all tenure in 1981, to 67.8% in 1992, and council tenancies decreased from 28.9% to 19.8% over the same period. Private renting has been in decline since before the first world war when about 90% of households in the UK rented from private landlords. By 1939 this was 65%, in 1981 9%, and 7.4% in 1992. In 1974 unskilled manual workers comprised 12% of owner occupiers but this had increased to 24% by 1984.

This restructuring has brought with it many social problems in all sectors. For some people owner occupation has brought security, better conditions and a capital asset which could appreciate. However home ownership for others on low incomes has been less beneficial. High interest rates and low inflation have brought home the reality of ownership as costs of repair and maintenance have increased.

In the main it is the better council houses which have been sold, so that the condition of the remainder is poor, and harder to maintain — much of it is unmodernised pre-second world war property. However it is the problems of the disastrous 1960s high-rise, deck-access and system build properties which predominate. They need major renovation and environmental improvements and in some cases structural enhancement.

Associated with the loss of the better off property from the public sector has been the loss of more affluent tenants, leaving a higher proportion of people who are poor, unemployed, and generally disadvantaged or vulnerable. This 'residualisation' increases the image, fostered by the Conservatives, of council housing as being 'second best', and only for those people who are unable or unwilling to 'help themselves'.

Large council estates are now suffering from the effects of a concentration of seriously disadvantaged or vulnerable tenants and this

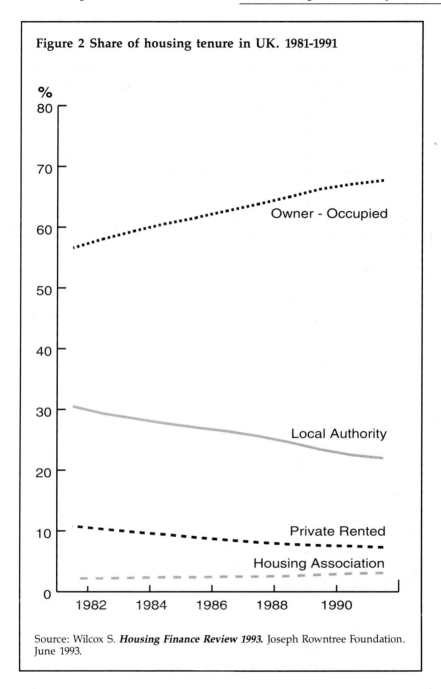

Figure 2 Share of housing tenure in UK. 1981-1991

Owner - Occupied

Local Authority

Private Rented

Housing Association

Source: Wilcox S. *Housing Finance Review 1993.* Joseph Rowntree Foundation. June 1993.

serves to depress whole communities. Others, perhaps with roots in the community, are now unwilling to live or buy property there, further increasing the homogeneity of poverty, or ghettoisation, of these estates.

A mixed tenure system is important, both for social reasons and for providing an excess of rented accommodation allowing for mobility and real choice. Most other European countries, although increasing their owner-occupied sector, have not based their policies on the development of this sector alone.

Owner occupation in some other European countries[6]	
England	68%
Denmark	52%
France	51%
Austria	50%
Netherlands	43%
Sweden	39%
Switzerland	30%

Issues in the housing crisis

While Conservative housing policies may have appeared to benefit some sections of the population they have also had disastrous consequences, not only for those in greatest poverty but also for other sections of the population. Here we look briefly at some of those consequences:

- housing shortages;
- homelessness;
- deterioration of houses;
- reduced access to housing;
- government control over the management of public housing;
- the increase in housing costs.

Housing needs and shortage of affordable housing

In crude terms there appears to be a surplus of one million dwellings over households in England and Wales. However, 1.4 million

(7.4%) houses are unfit.[7] It is also estimated that 1.2 million households need accommodation where individuals or couples are currently sharing with another host household and would prefer to live separately.[8]

Estimates of housing need are based on demographic trends. The number of households in the UK is increasing. (Table VIII)

Table VIII Number of Households 1961 — 1991, UK[9]				
Year	1961	1971	1981	1991
Total households (thousands)	16,189	18,317	19,492	21,897
1 person households (as a % of all housing tenures)	12%	18%	22%	27%

Some reasons for this increase are:
- household formation by the children of the 1960s baby boom, estimated to contribute 90,000 a year in the early 1990s;
- an increase in the number of one person households;
- separation and divorce, approximately 80,000 households a year;
- an increase in the numbers of elderly people.

Future estimates suggest an increase in households of 15% in England between 1991 and 2011,[10] including an increase in the number of one person households.

Private housing does not alleviate social need. Affordable rented accommodation (social housing) is therefore fundamental to the housing system. A survey in 1991 found that *'access to owner occupation remains a very substantial problem for new younger households, with only 29% able to buy a new home, and less than half (45%) able to afford a suitable home'*.[11] The reports continues *'as many as 38% of new younger households have little option but to rent ... half or more of new households require some form of social housing provision'*. In addition, to allow for mobility so that people can move, for example for reasons of work, there needs to be an excess of dwellings over households, particularly rented accommodation.[12]

Several estimates of the required number of social housing units have been made.[13] The National Housing Forum, the Institute of Housing, and the Audit Commission consider that some 80,000 housing units are required each year. This figure is based on inadequate provision within existing stock together with a forecast of household growth. It does not make any allowance for single person households.

Others estimate that 100,000 social houses are required each year to cover the number that are inadequately housed. This estimate includes households who are currently unable to afford home ownership or gain access to the social sector, and tenure flows within the housing stock together with private sector investment.[14]

In May 1993 Sir George Young, the Minister responsible for housing, said that housing associations would be enabled to provide 170,000 new social homes over the three years from 1992/93 (this would mean 57,000 units a year).[15]

Government response to housing shortages

Conservative governments since 1979 have firmly, and consistently, rejected planning techniques to determine future housing need in favour of its market and intuitive — 'what the country can afford' — philosophy. However the importance of housing for society, together with the time required for building and modifying properties, means that overall planning is crucial to securing sufficient appropriate accommodation in the years ahead. It cannot be left to a laissez-faire experiment. Housing completions for different housing tenures, shown in figure 3, confirm the Government's approach.

The Government is promoting housing associations as the new providers of social housing. In 1991/92 housing associations accounted for 40% of total social housing investment compared with 12% in 1979/80. However housing associations still represent only 4% of the housing tenure, and cannot compensate for the loss of rented accommodation in the council or private sectors.

Increasingly housing associations are required to raise more money from private investors. In 1974 a capital grant (Housing Association Grant, HAG) was introduced which covered 85% of most housing schemes and, 100% of many special needs developments. Legislation in 1989 reduced that to 72%, with the rest raised privately. By 1995 it will be reduced again to 55% and many believe that institutional investors will not be prepared to invest the remainder against the security of a tenanted home.[16] Higher levels of private funding will mean dramatic rent increases to service the higher level of private investment.

In response to these changes the Housing Corporation (a

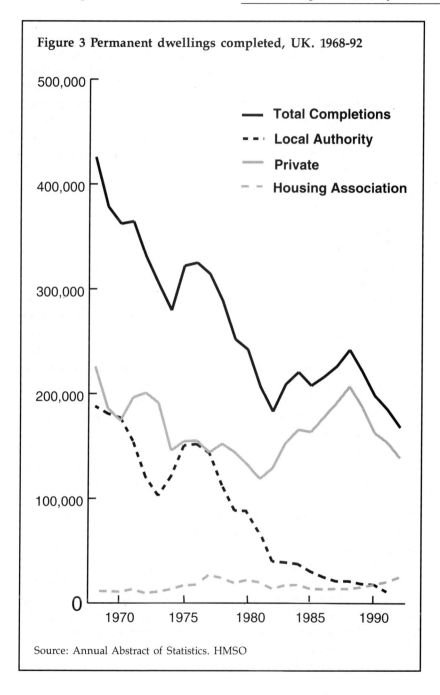

Figure 3 Permanent dwellings completed, UK. 1968-92

Source: Annual Abstract of Statistics. HMSO

government quango which allocates these government grants) is to reduce the housing associations who receive the grant from over 600 to under 100, restricting funding to the most financially sound.

A recent report found that large housing association estates, which are being built as a result of government encouragement, are housing seriously disadvantaged tenants, creating unbalanced communities and the likelihood of future expensive social problems.[17] *'Estates like this are already experiencing most of the social problems associated with run down council estates, despite being only about four years old'.*[18]

Homelessness

One of the most visible, and tragic, consequences of the shortage of affordable housing is the rapid increase in homelessness. The word suggests a range of images from people sleeping rough on the streets of London, to families in bed and breakfast, or sharing accommodation with another household.

Official homelessness however has a narrow definition and refers only to those people who apply to, and are accepted by, local authorities under the law as homeless. They are households, often families with children, who are considered to be homeless **and** in priority need **and** not intentionally homeless **and** to have a connection to the area. Local authorities are not obliged to rehouse single people or childless couples, and these are not included in the official figures.

Only a third of the 390,000 people who applied for a home in 1992 were accepted as homeless. The shortage of local authority housing is a reason for a stricter interpretation of the law.

Homeless households in England increased from 57,200 in 1979, to 151,720 in 1991. There were 148,250 in 1992 following a revised system of recording from 1 April 1991.[19] (figure 4)

About two thirds of the **official homeless** of England are outside London. The rate of increase in homelessness has been greater outside the capital over the last twenty-five years.[20] (Table IX)

Homelessness in rural areas tripled in the four years to 1992,[22] and overall it has increased faster than urban homelessness. The young, single, and new households are unable to afford accommodation and tend to leave rural areas, where a more restrictive interpretation of the law may be used.[23] Reports of people sleeping rough in the countryside are now widespread.

In Scotland homelessness has risen by 75% in the last 10 years.

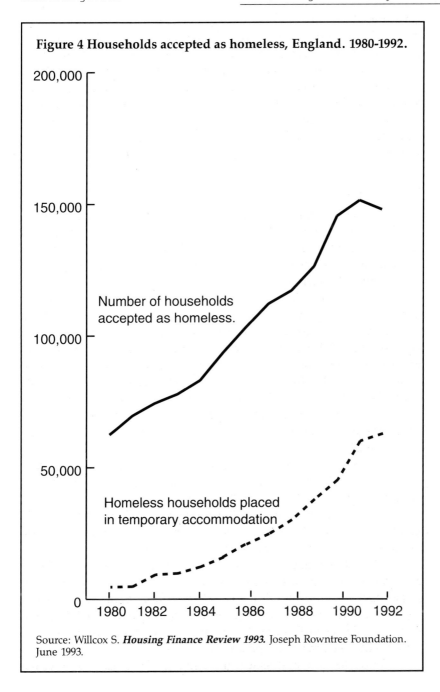

Figure 4 Households accepted as homeless, England. 1980-1992.

Number of households accepted as homeless.

Homeless households placed in temporary accommodation

Source: Willcox S. *Housing Finance Review 1993.* Joseph Rowntree Foundation. June 1993.

Table IX Percentage growth in official homelessness 1985 — 1990[21]		
	Total increase (%)	Average annual increase (%)
Inner London	43.0	7.0
Outer London	55.7	9.3
Metropolitan districts	83.8	14.0
Non-metropolitan districts	72.0	12.0
All England	74.5	12.4

Source: Kettlewell, J. *Public Finance and Accountancy*. May 1992.

Between 1983 and 1990 actual homelessness increased by 95% in Scottish rural areas and by 150% in 'remote ' Scotland.

Homelessness among physically disabled people increased by 92% between 1980 and 1986 compared to a 57% increase in homelessness among all types of household.[24]

Because of the lack of social housing local authorities are increasingly having to use temporary accommodation while waiting for permanent homes to become available. One local authority warns that if the decline in the number of 2/3 bed houses continues, by 1995 they will be unable to meet their obligations to homeless families.[25] The overcrowded and dangerous conditions of much bed and breakfast accommodation are well known. Kitchens, toilets and bathrooms on different floors and up dangerous staircases are often shared by several other families.

The term 'temporary accommodation' is an understatement. In 1987 the average period of stay was 33 weeks, and a third of families were there for over a year. In 1991 the average length of stay in London was 47 weeks, and 37% of households were in temporary accommodation for over a year, and 7% for over two years.

The costs of official homelessness

The cost of homelessness in England and Wales in 1991-92 was £193 million, and of this £121.8 million was spent by London Boroughs (these figures exclude the cost of accommodation secured in local authority property).[26]

Shelter asks if this is value for money compared with the cost of providing council housing. (See Table X).

Table X Value for money?[27]		
	Cost of Bed and Breakfast	Cost of Council Housing
Average annual cost per family/home	£13,150	£7,000
Total annual cost for 11,080 families	£146 million	£78 million
Estimated annual saving from ending B & B	£68 million	
	Cost of Private Sector Leasing	Cost of Council Housing
Average annual cost per family/home	£11,000	£7,000
Total annual cost for 26,460 families	£291 million	£185 million
Estimated annual saving from ending private sector leasing	£106 million	—
Total annual estimated saving from ending use of bed and breakfast and private sector leasing	£174 million	—

Note: The above estimates are based on the best and most up-to-date sources of information available but they are estimates only and should be treated as such. Assessment of relative costs are very susceptible to changes in interest rates, house prices, retail prices, etc.

Source: Burrows L, Walentowicz P. *Homes Cost Less than Homelessness.* Shelter 1992. p23.

Unofficial homelessness

Shelter has estimated the number of unofficial homeless (single people and childless couples) living in various types of accommodation. (See Table XI)

In 1989 the University of Surrey estimated that there were 75,000 homeless people in London, of whom 18,000 were in hostels and 2,000 were on the streets. Of the people on the streets 30% were over the age of 50 years.[29]

**Table XI Estimate of 'unofficial homeless':
actual and potential, 1990s, England[28]**

Description	Estimate of numbers
People sleeping rough	up to 8,000 (Shelter estimate)
Unauthorised tenants/squatters	up to 50,000 (Shelter estimate) of whom 31,000 are in London
Single people in hostels	up to 60,000 (1991 DoE)
Single people in lodgings	up to 77,000 (1989 DSS)
Insecure private tenants	up to 317,000 (1992 OPCS)
*Hidden homeless people	up to 1,200,000 (Shelter estimate)
Total	1,712,000

* These are people and households living with others when they would prefer to live separately.

Information obtained from: Department of the Environment (DoE)
Department of Social Security (DSS)
Office of Population Censuses and Surveys (OPCS)
Shelter

Source: Burrows L, Walentowicz P. **Homes Cost Less Than Homelessness.**
Shelter. 1992. p23.

As a result of spending nearly £100 million in London on the Rough Sleepers Initiative (RSI), several thousand people have been provided with accommodation bringing the numbers down to about 400. However the rate at which increased hostel and shelter provision filled up demonstrated a serious need for 'move-on' accommodation, including supported accommodation. The evaluation concluded that the RSI should continue and be extended outside London.[30] However the Government sees investment in RSI as a short term measure.

About a third of homeless rough sleepers and common lodging house dwellers have severe mental health problems. The number of psychiatric beds in England has fallen from 148,000 in 1954 to about 45,000 in 1992. Schizophrenic men who are lost to follow-up after being in hospital, do become homeless.[31] The lack of low cost rented accommodation and the difficulty of admitting acutely ill patients under the 1983 Mental Health Act, may be more significant for the high numbers of psychiatrically disturbed people among the homeless, than the de-institutionalisation of long stay patients with learning difficulties.[32]

Deteriorating stock

The building standards of new properties are carefully prescribed by building regulations and by-laws. There have also been a series of influential reports from government committees that have set standards for new council housing — the Tudor Walters Committee (1918), the Dudley Committee (1944) and the Parker Morris Committee (1961). In 1980 however the Government abolished the Parker Morris standards allowing each authority to decide its own standards. The Institute of Housing and the Royal Institute of British Architects, among others, expressed their concerns about the abolition of minimum space and amenity standards *'at a time of extreme economic restraint, it is more important than ever to seek value for money in the provision of new housing. The new project control system recently introduced for local authority housing is based on this concept yet fails to make allowance for high standards which a local authority may wish to achieve for social reasons or to reduce longer term maintenance costs'.*[33]

However new building adds little to the total housing stock in any one year (less than 2%), and new building standards therefore have only very long term effects. The major problem is the disrepair of the current ageing and unsuitable housing stock. From the end of the first world war until the 1960s many people benefited from being rehoused from slum areas into new, higher standard, accommodation. However many more would have benefited if their existing homes had been upgraded.

Scale of the problem

In 1989 the Association of District Councils (a Conservative controlled organisation) estimated that the cost to the public sector of repairing the unfit private sector was £9.7 billion. It suggested a ten year programme costing £970 million a year to do this. In addition £2,000 million a year would be needed for ten years to improve the public sector housing stock.[34] These figures do not include replacement of demolished properties which would cost a further £3,300 million a year for ten years.[35]

The first Scottish House Condition Survey published in 1993 found that 30% (584,000) of Scottish dwellings were damp, and 94,000 were below the tolerable standard. Using new fitness standards the 1991 English House Conditions Survey found 1,456,000 (7.4%) of homes were unfit.

The owner occupied sector had the largest number of unfit properties. Many people who were encouraged to buy in the late 1980s during the credit boom are now realising the reality of entering the property market. People on fixed incomes such as pensions, or those made redundant, or unemployed, are often unable to keep up mortgage payments or to improve or maintain their properties.

The huge reductions in investment in social housing, along with the better properties having been sold, has resulted in a massive backlog of disrepair and deteriorating council housing stock.

However the properties in most serious disrepair remain within the private rented sector (although this is the smallest sector). The English House Conditions Survey shows that 20% of this sector is unfit, and that one in five tenants are not living in decent conditions. Houses in multiple occupation (HMOs) are in the worst condition. To repair and upgrade the 300,000 HMOs in England and Wales would cost, at 1985 prices, £3.6 billion.

The Government's response

Legislation covering standards of existing dwellings was not enacted until an 'unfitness standard' was established in 1957. This was based almost entirely on a government 'manual' of 1919 which, even then, represented only the minimum standards. This was finally updated in 1990, acknowledging the existence of artificial lighting, heating, and indoor baths and toilets. Even so it *still lags many decades behind people's expectations*.[36] The 1990 standards still fail to recognise internal room arrangements and energy conservation and *'the clear evidence of the central importance of warmth and lack of dampness in houses for health is not recognised, despite the changes'*.[37]

Whereas the 1957 unfitness standards were meant as a device for authorities to start compulsory purchase orders, their 1990 equivalent was brought in to 'target', and thereby limit, grants available for home improvement.

The Local Government and Housing Act 1989 was partly designed to simplify the system of giving grants to the private sector and establish a new framework for tackling 'Renewal Areas'. It introduced a stringent means-test for owner occupiers applying for grants, so that only those on the lowest incomes receive a full grant and those with modest means start to pay substantial contributions. Grants were made mandatary, payable by local authorities but from very limited funds. Most authorities do not advertise the grants for fear of creating a demand they cannot meet. There were 219,800 improvement grants in 1983 but only 34,000 in 1992.

The 1989 legislation did not address the worsening problems of disrepair in all sectors, especially those in the worst properties. Mobile homes and caravans are exempt from unfitness standards and buildings controls. For many living in the poorest public and owner occupier sectors existing laws do not apply, and those living in houses of multiple occupation also find that authorities are unable to enforce the standards. Meanwhile the Government continues to cut investment. According to the Institute of Housing the budget for improvements will decrease from £346 million in 1993/4 to £260 million in 1994/5.[38]

The Government requires authorities to bid for a limited amount of credit borrowing capacity to undertake schemes which meet certain government defined standards. Authorities are using this 'Estate Action' money in imaginative and constructive ways. However again, heavy central control and limited resources mean that it is hardly sufficient to contribute to an overall improvement to the council stock.

Housing associations are being encouraged to assist in inner city renewal work. But, as with their building programme, the introduction of the need for increased private finance, together with the Housing Corporation's fixation on very specific criteria for 'value-for-money', means that many associations are unable to take part in such schemes.

Area clearance schemes are one solution authorities might wish to adopt, but financial constraints again prevent this action, along with the real costs of compensation, the lack of available alternative accommodation and the difficulty of maintaining communities.

Access to social housing on medical grounds

Only a few people are rehoused on medical grounds, amounting to 4% of housing applicants,[39] [40] although the demand varies from 17%,[41] to 70% of all applicants.[42] Even so, in 1988 new tenants with medical priority waited an average of two years before being rehoused.[43]

Methods of assessment vary and, according to a survey of 55 large public landlords:
- 29% depended on self assessment by the applicant;
- 22% on the opinion of the general practitioner;
- 25% on the findings of trained housing visitors;
- the remainder on assessments made by housing officers.[44]

Sometimes more than one method was used.

There are no guidelines for doctors in assessment of 'housing related' medical conditions. Most GPs do not know how the housing system works and its limitations in providing accommodation. A study in 1986 showed that GPs were not interested in, nor were they concerned to modify, local housing policy.[45]

After assessment there are three main systems for prioritising applicants:

- a points system (55%);[46]
- the identification of needy groups, each of which has a quota of allocations (28%);
- waiting lists based on date of application (8%).

Parsons[47] considers the idea of medical priority as immoral. It raises expectations unduly in that it fraudulently offers the possibility of housing when the reality is against such an offer being made. It uses a lot of community medicine time and the process can be used to hide the effects of the cuts in housing investment.

Suggestions to improve the system have been put forward,[48 49] including a points system for integrating disabled people into a housing allocations system.[50]

A new approach

In Newcastle-upon-Tyne, collaboration between housing departments, social services departments, the health authority and researchers, is directed at allocation and investment priorities. The aim is to produce certain social and health gains directly, or to play a part in a range of services for improving the circumstances of individual households.[51] The effects of the neighbourhood are included in assessing medical need and health gains from rehousing. This is important where health problems, including stress and fear, are associated with the community or neighbourhood, unlike the usual assessments which emphasise the health status of the individual.

In a proposed Neighbourhood Renewal Area validated questionnaires were used to ask about health, including mental health. Respondents were also asked to rank how stressful their life was. The stress levels were found to be a good indicator of psychiatric distress. Applicants for rehousing were most likely to be suffering most stress. By concentrating joint assessments on those on the housing waiting lists simple practical contributions to reduce some of the worst effects of the house could be made, for example measures to reduce damp and to increase protection against burglary.

Disability and access to housing

It is estimated that more than three quarters of a million physically handicapped people in Britain are inadequately housed, and the National Federation of Housing Associations estimate that there is a shortfall of 150,000 purpose built, or suitably modified, houses in the public sector.

Most disabled people depend on local authorities for access to housing. This has been provided directly by the local authority although the Government intends that in the future the main provider will be housing associations. Housing is also indirectly provided by local authorities, by means of the improvement grant system for adaptations to private accommodation. Most wheelchair housing, and the majority of mobility housing, is owned by local authorities. By restricting local authority investment in special needs housing, central Government has exacerbated the existing inadequate provision for disabled people.

The future of small housing associations who cater for the needs of special groups is at risk under the proposed financial changes which will reduce the amount of financial support the Government will provide to housing associations. Also, under the new mixed funding system, general needs housing associations without a special interest in the disabled have been building developments which have lower space standards.

A study in 1990 asked 21 local authorities in England and Wales about the housing, and housing related, needs of disabled people in their area.[52] Most had little knowledge of the demand for housing which existed among disabled people, or what, if any, appropriate housing existed. There were few strategies addressing the needs of disabled people. For example wheelchair access was not included in private sector partnership agreements. Co-ordination between housing and social services was infrequent and few social services departments had policies on independent living.

In the opinion of the report's author, Dr Jenny Morris, central government, particularly through the Department of the Environment and the Housing Corporation, has a critical role to play, by using regulatory and financial powers to promote the interests of disabled people. She called for the adoption by housing associations and private developers of criteria such as level access, wider doorways, ground floor WCs, and barrier free external environments as minimum standards, together with a requirement to build a percentage of dwellings to the 'housing for disabled people' standard.

Figure 5 Specialised dwellings for chronically sick and disabled. England. 1981-1992.

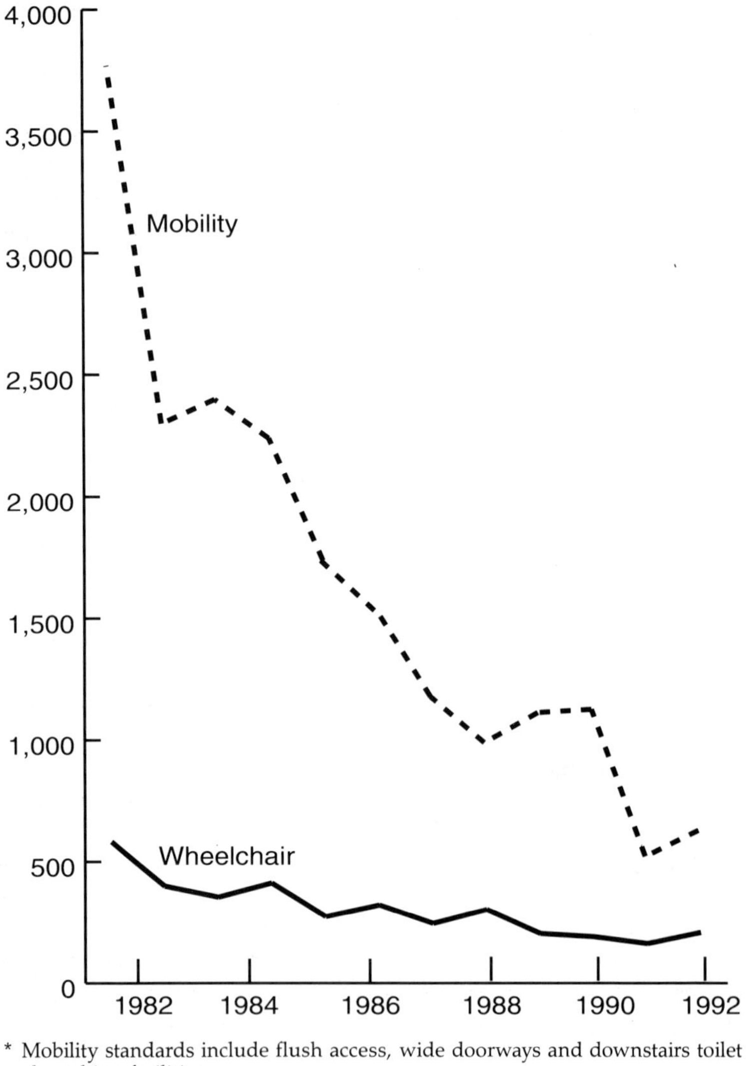

* Mobility standards include flush access, wide doorways and downstairs toilet and washing facilities.

Source: Department of the Environment. HMSO. London
Housing and Construction Statistics

> Among the few examples of good practice is the Derbyshire Centre for Integrated Living, a centre for disabled people, staffed mainly by them, and which has a register of adapted housing in the district. The London Borough of Islington has adopted a policy on provision of housing for the disabled which sets down that 25% of all newbuild dwellings are to be built to 'housing for people with disabilities' standards', and the rest to 'mobility housing standard'. Similar policies apply to estates. All housing association schemes are scrutinised by the Design Sub-Group of the Housing for Disabled People Group before being presented for council approval.

Accountability and control

Much of the reaction to the Conservative onslaught on local authorities over the last decade has centred less on policy issues and more on the management or organisational issues of running housing departments. Various solutions have been put forward, and enacted, including decentralisation of services, equal opportunities policies, tenant management of estates, and other tenant participation initiatives.

However, many of the initiatives have been based on private sector management practices. The Audit Commission, set up by the Government to investigate the running of public bodies, has reported on the 'Three Es' — economy, efficiency and effectiveness.[53] This emphasis has encouraged the growth of other — originally market oriented — initiatives to be implemented, such as customer care, Total Quality Management and customer satisfaction surveys.

Given its vendetta against local authorities, the Government had a problem. How could it strengthen its influence over a service which is essentially managed through local officers? The solution has been to impose compulsory competitive tendering (CCT) on the management of council housing.

The Government is really only concerned with the property management functions of housing and in running council services along business lines, believing in the ability of the market to provide services economically and flexibly. Any social objectives are lost. *'Greater competition is the best way of securing greater efficiency, while guaranteeing a high standard of service to the tax payer'.*[54] (The Secretary of State for the Environment, 1993.)

Housing management is a personal service in which an officer-

---

Compulsory Competitive Tendering Arrangements

Most of the housing management functions which are presently carried out by the local authority, will have to be put out to tender. Services include:

- collecting rents, arrears and service charges;
- allocating properties, enforcing tenancy agreements;
- management of vacant properties, repairs and maintenance;
- day to day housing management;
- caretaking and cleaning.

The council will retain central key policy functions.

The lowest bidder from amongst potential contractors (such as housing associations, estate agents, housing consultants, private contractors, in-house local authorities or management buy-outs) will take over parts of the housing management services on a contracted out basis.

In setting out CCT there is an emphasis on the importance of consulting tenants and involving them in housing management. However under CCT tenants will have no right of veto over a contract and therefore current legislation, ensuring they have that right, will be changed.

The Government has decided to go ahead without waiting for the results of 7 pilot projects. The first contracts must be operating by April 1996.

---

tenant relationship is often built on a local understanding of the area and a basic trust for the council generally. The housing managers' and officers' role can be more than that of the rent collector; they can have a considerable social and health value. It is difficult to see how these roles can be built into a 'for profit' contract, particularly at a time of low investment of resources in house building and repairs.

Opposition to the introduction of CCT has been widespread. Various housing and local authorities, including the Conservative run Association of District Councils, are opposed to the compulsory nature of the proposals, and are not convinced that CCT will improve quality or cost-effectiveness. Tenants have protested against CCT, especially against the reduction of their current rights to veto contracts. Tenants also fear they will have to pay the extra costs involved.

Local authorities, however, are a form of government responsible to a local electorate. They should reflect the concerns and issues of those living and working in its area, seeking to meet local need, and giving local people an opportunity to have access to decision making that affects their lives. They should not be run purely as a private sector organisation.

The Government has done all it can to remove these principles, to remove local control, power, accountability, and to reduce the function of local authorities to that of administering a series of contracts every few years based on a coordinating role.

We therefore need to address the genuine problems of managing many of the larger authorities and difficult estates in a way that does not compromise our Socialist beliefs. Management needs to be founded on principles such as equal opportunities, real tenant involvement, freedom of choice and full tenants rights. New forms of management should be developed and encouraged through proper resourcing and monitoring. Locally based, flexible and responsive initiatives need to be devised, such as tenant management co-operatives, Estate Management Boards and local housing companies. Also inter-sectoral collaboration between departments and agencies should be encouraged at all levels.

The Cost of Housing

The Government claims to be concerned with enhancing choice for people. However freedom of choice in housing is not a right which can be generally enjoyed by people with low incomes and resources, even when they are owners. Choice in this context means that those who have resources and the ability to pay can choose, whereas those without resources have little, if any, choice.

Irrespective of type of tenure, housing costs account for a larger proportion of the total weekly expenditure of the low-income families than of higher income families.[55]

Other government policies, such as high interest rates and the poll tax, have left low income households worse off, making it even more difficult for them to obtain the housing they need and pay the costs of living there.

Owner occupation

There is a stereotype of the owner occupier as that of the middle or upper income group buying a suburban or non-flatted dwelling using a single variable rate mortgage secured from a building society with the loan being repaid after 25 years or on movement. In reality the picture is more complex.

In 1990 research showed that one in six owners had an income of less than £5,200.[56] Some 7% of all owners sampled were in receipt of housing benefit and this proportion rose to over 40% for owners with incomes below £5,200. The research found 25% of owners were over 60 years of age in 1988. This group were disproportionately (18%) supported by housing benefit, indeed the vast majority of elderly people with a live mortgage receive housing benefit.

Although Mortgage Income Tax Relief support is given to all mortgage payers regardless of their financial circumstances, social security help is available for mortgage interest payments only to those on income support. This causes a huge poverty trap for people on low incomes who just fail to qualify for income support. As a result, many owner occupiers in low paid work are forced to choose between losing their homes or giving up their jobs. A solution to this would be the introduction of a 'mortgage benefit' similar to the housing benefit scheme. Such a scheme would cost about £820 million annually.[57]

Many households are now living in properties worth less than their mortgage; at the end of 1992 the properties of 1.3 million households were worth on average £2,800 less than their outstanding mortgage.[58]

Mortgage repossessions and arrears

Between 1981 and June 1992, 300,000 households had their homes repossessed; over half since the start of 1990.[59] Repossessions are just the tip of an iceberg of growing numbers of home owners who are falling into serious arrears. Indeed the recent fall in the number of houses repossessed is likely to be reversed with 'recovery' in the housing market.[60]

In a study of people who had lost their homes, or were in arrears, Ford's findings *suggest that there is likely to be a permanent growth in the demand for rental property'*. The majority of those who now live in shared or rented accommodation are increasingly looking to become, or remain, tenants, and those in arrears *'showed little commitment to home ownership'*.[61]

Rents

The cost of rented accommodation has increased dramatically. In the period 1982/1983 to 1988/1989 rents in the public rented sector went up by 39.2%, housing association rents increased by 56.1% and

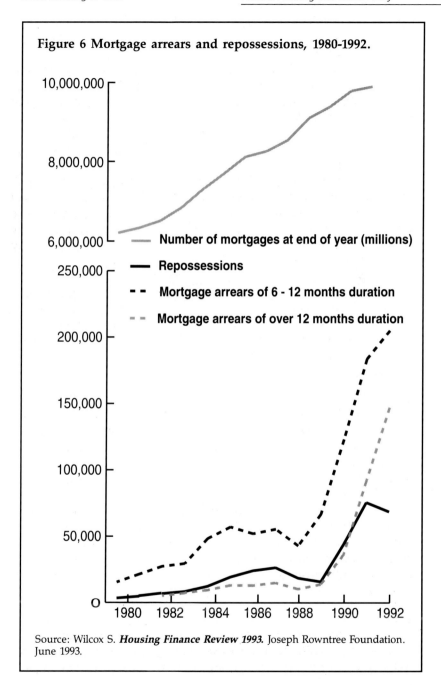

Figure 6 Mortgage arrears and repossessions, 1980-1992.

Source: Wilcox S. *Housing Finance Review 1993.* Joseph Rowntree Foundation. June 1993.

those of the private sector increased by 69.8%. As the cost of rented accommodation has increased tenants have become relatively poorer. 70% of all tenants (both public and private) now receive housing benefit.

Rents have continued to rise in the early 1990s, largely as a result of the 1988 Housing Act's shift to 'market rents' and the Government's reduction in social housing subsidies. This has led to rent increases in the private sector, precluding access to much of it by low income households.

Average housing association rents for all new lettings rose 2.5 times the rate of inflation between 1989 to 1991, despite some of the rents being subsidised by associations. For working tenants moving into these lettings the average weekly income after rent and other basic living costs had been paid, fell from £41 to £35 between these years.[62] Most of this fall is due to new housing association funding arrangements and the Government's implicit assumption that working tenants should pay 33% of their incomes on rent. The National Federation of Housing Associations believe a more realistic figure should be 22%.

The rented sector generally provides housing for tenants on less than average incomes, and an increasing proportion of these tenants are on low incomes.[63] In an article looking at 'affordability' Hancock found that a significant number of council tenants are falling completely through the welfare net. They are having to pay large increases in rents without any access to housing benefit.[64]

Housing benefit is a means-tested benefit, or income related payment, given to low income tenants to help with their rent. Households in receipt of income support (or whose income is at or below that level) receive the maximum assistance. Council tenants receive a rebate, other tenants a rent allowance in the form of a direct cash payment.

The Government estimates that just over 4.6 million households will receive housing benefit during 1993/94 — about 62% of all tenants. Housing benefit accounts for 2% of all public expenditure, and about 10% of the social security budget. Benefit payments in 1993/94 are expected to cost £8,000 million.

The housing benefit scheme has been used by the Conservative Government to cloak the worst effects of their high rent/low investment policies. It has enabled them to reduce public investment in homes, yet claiming to help the poorest. However spending on housing benefit rose appreciably in the early 1980s, stabilised in the mid to late 1980s, and is now rising again. It rose, not because benefits became more generous, but because the economic recession has led to higher unemployment and an increase in the number of recipients, and also because of the increases in rents in the public and private sector.

The increased cost of housing benefit diminished government savings from reduced investment in housing. The Government therefore instituted a series of savage cuts in the housing benefit system.

Housing Benefit Poverty Trap

Households with an income above the income support threshold, may still be entitled to housing benefit but at a reduced level which tapers according to their income. A household in work therefore may find that an increase in earnings leaves them little better off because of the extra tax and national insurance contributions they need to pay and the loss in benefit they incur, as a result of earning more.

This effect can reduce work incentives and the differentials in net income over a range of earnings. People can become trapped in poverty, unable to improve their position by working more.

Between 1983 and 1987 a number of increases were made to the income levels used in calculating the amount of housing benefit. A total of 1.5 million households, including 660,000 pensioners, lost all entitlement to housing benefit as a result of these changes (Hansard, 20 December 1985 and 19 December 1986, cols 410-412 and 697-700).

The Government claimed that further changes made in 1988 would reduce the number of recipients, including those receiving rate rebates only, by around one million people and would achieve systemic savings in benefit expenditure of about £640 million (Hansard 18 December 1987 cols 887-888).

It has been estimated that as many as 900,000 people may fail to claim their benefits and that £900 million a year is going unclaimed. The Conservative Government has discouraged campaigns to improve the uptake of benefits.

Conclusions

Housing in the 1990s is in crisis. This may not be immediately obvious to the majority of households who are well housed, have good prospects of improving their situation, and for whom the current state system operates to safeguard market conditions. The crisis is more apparent to the growing minority who do not have a home, who are dependent on a declining and deliberately run-down social housing sector, and who are reliant on ever decreasing means tested hand-outs.

With this growing residential polarisation between sections of our society come greater social and economic inequalities, and an increased incidence of the health related issues. Homelessness, poor standards of housing, deteriorating environmental and social circumstances, inadequate choice of affordable or physically suitable accommodation, loss of individual and locally collective control over one's housing environment, and the stress of living with financial inequalities, all contribute to the crisis.

The shift of government emphasis from subsidising bricks and mortar in the social sector to the capital investment of owner occupiers has considerably increased the hardship and social segregation of the poorer sections of the population. Ironically, however, larger portions of public money are spent in administering means-tested 'hand-outs' to help the poor.

3 Towards an equitable housing strategy

The lack of sufficient affordable decent housing is a public health issue. Decent housing and an equitable housing strategy are essential for health.

An equitable housing policy should be based on an appreciation of:

- the fundamental need for shelter;
- secure and safe accommodation;
- real choice of tenure;
- some autonomy and control over one's housing situation.

Simple shelter is not enough in an advanced urban society. The aspiration to decent housing should not only be acknowledged but enshrined as a legal right in a Housing Rights Act. The Housing Rights Act would establish the right to secure, decent, affordable housing for all households — including single person households — irrespective of tenure.

The Government must ensure the implementation of such rights through the fair and equitable provision of resources at local level.

The aims of such an equitable housing policy would be to:
- provide sufficient social housing;
- provide social housing of a decent quality;
- promote real choice of housing tenure;
- promote local democracy in a comprehensive housing service;
- address inequalities related to housing.

Sufficient social housing

Accommodation must be provided for all who want it, including people presently classified as officially and unofficially homeless. This requires the provision of an additional 100,000 social rented housing units a year over the next 10 years.

Means to achieve this include:
- allowing local authorities to use all the capital receipts from the sale of council houses for re-investment in social housing;
- a rehabilitation programme for the thousands of private, council, housing association and government-owned homes which currently lie empty;[1]
- the purchase of privately owned properties by local authorities;
- lifting the present restrictions on local authority expenditure on housing. Local authorities should be permitted higher limits on borrowing for capital investment and be allowed to borrow for housing investment on the same terms as housing associations or private developers;
- taking housing finance out of Public Sector Borrowing Requirement calculations.

House building is an effective way of creating jobs because it is a labour intensive industry. It is estimated that for every £20,000 invested in housing one new job is created. Each home built or improved would create two new jobs, one on site and one in the construction supplies industry. There would be savings on benefits and lost tax for each person gaining work.[1,2]

---

1. It is estimated that there are 640,000 empty privately owned properties and 35,000 empty government properties. The "big" mortgage lenders currently have 75,000 repossessed properties on their books.

Social housing of decent quality

The quality of housing in all tenures, including both existing property and new houses, must be improved. Minimum housing standards of fitness, which would include efficient heating and insulation, should be introduced. The quality of private rented accommodation should be improved through encouragement and enforcement of high standards, particularly of houses in multiple occupation and temporary accommodation.

The massive problems of disrepair in both the private and public sector must be addressed, with particular emphasis on the problems faced by poor elderly home owners.

Means to achieve this include:

- incorporating insulation, heating and safety features in the specifications for new buildings, and for renovations to existing property. Mobility, wheelchair, and similar access standards, together with adaptations to enable disabled people to live independently, should also be incorporated into greater proportions of new build and renovations.
- provision of entryphones, particularly for elderly people, handrails on stairs, efficient lifts, safe children's play areas, community halls available to people on large estates, arrangements for organised parking and efficient rubbish collection, pleasant common garden areas.
- subsidising Care and Repair, Stay Put, and similar schemes to help people maintain and remain in their homes;
- resourcing local authorities adequately so that they can repair their own property and give tenants access to caretakers with ability to arrange repairs, maintenance and the cleaning of common areas. Local authorities should be enabled to offer a repair service to homeowners, either by direct labour, or by providing advice about using private contractors. Local authorities should be able to give realistic improvement grants by using higher means test levels and larger grants.
- encouraging clearance programmes by providing local authorities with money, so that they can develop areas sensitively taking community issues into account.

Choice of housing tenure

For real choice there must be sufficient good quality houses across the range of housing tenures. To enable people to move there needs to be a surplus of decent affordable accommodation, especially in the rented sector, and a good tenure mix. Polarisation between tenures must be stopped.

Means to achieve this include:
- encouraging other forms of tenure and experimental ideas such as shared ownership, ownership co-operatives, local housing companies and self build schemes;
- helping people who feel burdened by the responsibility of home ownership, including the right to sell their home to the local authority and remain in it as a tenant.
- provision of sheltered accommodation and groundfloor flats in mixed developments, to enable elderly people to remain close to their relatives;
- provision of houses for families, with access to open space.

Local democracy in a comprehensive housing service

Central government's intervention in local aspects of housing must be reduced. The facilitating role of local government should be increased, to include both public and private sectors. At the same time the role of the local authority needs to change to enable citizen participation in the planning and delivery of housing services.

There should be strategic planning at local authority level and minimal overall co-ordination at government level. Planning in local areas should consider the whole needs of an area, including health, social, and educational needs.

There should be greater insistence on assessment of housing need. This should take into account needs expressed at the local housing area level. It should include research into the needs of vulnerable groups, as well as the monitoring of existing provision.

Means to achieve this include:

- restoration of the role and responsibility of accountable local authorities. Local authorities should not be compelled by central government to put housing management services out to competitive tendering.

- ensuring that local authorities and housing associations develop suitable tenant participation initiatives in co-operation with tenants' organisations. Such initiatives could include supporting tenants' associations, developing mechanisms for tenants to participate in the landlord's decision making process and promoting participative democracy through initiatives such as Tenant Management Organisations.

- participation in area regeneration and plans for housing should involve all local residents, to ensure provision of easy access to schools, libraries, day nurseries, health centres, shops and bus routes. Isolated local authority estates without amenities or shops are a threat to good health and social cohesiveness.

- local authorities taking a comprehensive, strategic, long term view of housing needs in the area. They are the appropriate body to do this and need to be sensitive to the needs of individual communities.

- supplementing this needs assessment by an audit of community level housing, which includes the needs of the disabled and the institutionalised, and should be assessed by and with them. Targets should be set for the assessment and provision of housing. Adequate resources to undertake such assessments should be available.

- making a separate assessment of the accommodation needs of young people, with their involvement. Because of the complex social and emotional needs of many young homeless people counselling and life skills training should be available for use by them as and when required. Initiatives such as 'foyers' should be explored.

- producing regional needs assessments and plans for housing on a regular (annual) basis. This information should be used to determine the national housing investment programme.

- enabling local authorities to establish non-profit making housing agencies which would provide a housing exchange service available to public and private tenants, and to owner occupiers. This would be linked to joint waiting lists and the ability of the local authorities to buy and sell property to break 'housing chains'. They would also act as holding bodies for returnable rent deposits, for people wishing to rent accommodation but who are unable to find a down payment.

- monitoring housing associations for accountability. Housing associations may not be accountable to tenants, especially as they are put under increasing financial pressure.
- monitoring and enforcing housing rights by certain functions of local authority housing departments.

Reducing housing inequalities

Inequality related to housing issues must be addressed and reversed through tax reforms and benefit changes. Also a legal system must be put in place to ensure that equality stemming from a fair fiscal policy is upheld.

The means of change would include:

- phasing out mortgage income tax relief. It must be replaced by some other form of housing needs related allowance. That allowance should include assistance with the costs of housing in use. The priority would be to help low income people with the costs of their accommodation regardless of tenure, including low income home owners.
- introducing a mortgage benefit scheme similar to the housing benefit scheme for people on low incomes with a mortgage who currently fail to qualify for income support and are consequently denied help with mortgage interest payments.
- tax reform to ensure a permanent reduction of speculation in the housing market. If necessary taxes should be increased to pay for social housing.
- reforming the housing revenue account to address inequalities in the current housing finance system and to prevent better off tenants paying the rebates of their poorer neighbours. Authorities could then set rents at affordable levels without making it necessary for two out of three tenants to claim means tested housing benefit. Since many tenants are on low incomes the case for means testing should be reviewed.

For greater equity mortgage interest tax relief MUST be reformed.

Alternatives to the present system of mortgage interest tax relief include some suggested by Aughton[3]:

- a gradual phasing out of mortgage income tax relief and its replacement by a housing needs related allowance which includes assistance with the cost of housing in use;
- tax relief could be given as at present but only for the first ten years of a mortgage;
- a 'single annuity' tax relief system. In such a system the first time buyer would get tax relief for the mortgage life, 25 years; if, say after 7 years, there was a move to another house, tax relief would be given on the new mortgage at year 8, not at year one, and so on ending altogether after 25 years;
- tax relief could be given to the cash value of the original mortgage.

It would be important to make sure that high earners could not switch to other forms of tax-deductible assistance provided by their employers.[4]

- reintroducing control and regulation of rents.
- reforming the present housing benefit scheme to increase the value of benefits and to improve benefit administration as suggested by Shelter and the Citizens Advice Bureau.[5]
- introducing safeguards to ensure the continuance of a more equitable housing system. With the introduction of a Housing Rights Act the housing court would hear cases of dispute about, and appeals in connection with, housing issues.
- establishing housing consumer councils to monitor housing standards in all tenures and review matters of housing affecting consumers and potential consumers. As a body separate from the providers, a housing inspectorate could be set up within the consumer council.
- restoring security of tenure for private rented and housing association tenants.

Conclusion

Decent affordable housing must be recognised as a pre-requisite for good health. Measures to address the disastrous consequences of the Conservative Government's housing policy are long overdue.

As Socialists we have a duty to ensure that all households have equal access to affordable housing, and ensure that they can afford to maintain and heat it. This will mean increasing capital investment in new-build as well as renovation and repairs, and in real management subsidies. It will mean ensuring adequate building and renovation standards, ensuring a well planned, comprehensive, local strategy, based on mixed tenure, and including real opportunities for participative democracy, and an enactment of housing rights for all.

References

Introduction

1 Social Trends, 1993, and Census 1991. OPCS. HMSO
2 Wilcox S. **Housing Finance Review, 1993.** Joseph Rowntree Foundation. June 1993.
3 Housing Review, Vol 42 No 1, January-February 1993 p1.
4 Aughton H. Malpass P. **Housing Finance: A Basic Guide.** Shelter. 1990.
5 Burrows L. Phelps L. Walentowicz P. **For Whose Benefit? The Housing Benefit Scheme Reviewed.** National Association of Citizens Advice Bureau and Shelter. 1993.
6 See Ref 2.
7 See Ref 2.
8 Hansard. Written reply, 23 February 1993. Col 522.
9 Annual Abstract of Statistics. **Permanent Dwellings Completed.** OPCS, HMSO.
10 Burrows L. Walentowicz P. **Homes Cost Less Than Homelessness.** Shelter. 1992. p22.
11 ibid
12 Wilcox S. **Housing the Hardest Cut to Make.** Inside Housing, 9 July 1993.
13 Department of the Environment. **English Housing Condition Survey, 1991. Preliminary Report on Unfit Dwellings.** HMSO. London. 1993.
14 Aughton H. **The Main Housing Problem, Contrived Amnesia.** Housing and Planning Review February/March 1992. p6.

15 *Households Below Average Income, A Statistical Analysis 1979 — 1990/91.* HMSO. 1993.

16 Quick A. Wilkinson R. *Income and Health*. Socialist Health Association. London. 1991.

17 Foster S. *Missing the Target*. Shelter Publications. 1993.

18 See Ref 10.

19 Whitehead C. Kleinman M. *A Review of Housing Needs Assessment*. Housing Corporation. 1992.

20 Local Government and Housing Act, 1989. HMSO.

21 See ref 4. p74.

22 *The Health of the Nation: A Strategy for Health in England*. HMSO. London. 1992.

1 Health and housing

1 Fox AJ, Goldblatt PO. *Longitudinal Study: Socio-demographic mortality differentials 1971-75*. Series LS No 1. HMSO London. 1982.

2 Hunt S. *'Damp & Mouldy Housing: A Holistic Approach'*. In *Unhealthy Housing*, Burridge R, Ormandy D (eds) E&FN Spon. London 1993.

3 Townsend P, Davidson N. *Inequalities in Health*. Penguin. London. 1992. p52.

4 Fox AJ, Jones DR, Goldblatt PO. *Approaches to studying the effect of socio-economic circumstances on geographic differences in mortality in England and Wales*. OPCS Longitudinal Study. Medical Bulletin 1984;40:4:309-314.

5 Goldblatt P. *'Mortality and Alternative Social Classifications'*. In *Longitudinal Study 1971-81: Mortality and Social Organisation*. Goldblatt P. (ed). OPCS LS series No. 6. HMSO. 1990.

6 Brennan ME, Lancashire R. *Association of Childhood Mortality with Housing Status and Unemployment*. Journal of Epidemiology and Community Health, 1978;32:28-33.

7 Macfarlane A, Mugford M. *Birth Counts: Statistics of Pregnancy and Childbirth*. National Perinatal Epidemiology Unit in Collaboration with OPCS. HMSO.1984.

8 Home Office. *Fire Statistics: United Kingdom*. HMSO. London. 1989.

9 Thomas A, Niner P. *Living in Temporary Accommodation: a Survey of Homeless People*. HMSO. London. 1989.

10 Keyes S, Kennedy M. *Sick to Death of Homelessness*. Crisis. London. December 1992.

11 Hansard. Written reply, 10 March 1993, col 633.

12 Quick A. *Unequal Risks: Accidents and Social Policy*. Socialist Health Association. London. 1991.

13 Department of Trade and Industry (DTI). *Home and Leisure Accident Research: Home Accident Surveillance System, Twelfth Annual Report, 1988 Data*. DTI Consumer Safety Unit. London. 1991.

14 Chandler SE, Chapman A, Hollington SJ. *Fire Incidence, Housing and Social Conditions — The Urban Situation in Britain*. Fire Prevention 1984;172:15-20.

15 Savage AV. *Warmth in winter: evaluation of an information pack for elderly people*. Cardiff: University of Wales College of Medicine Research Team for the Care of the Elderly. 1988.

16 Collins KV. *"Cold- and heat-related illnesses in the indoor environment."* In: *Unhealthy housing*. Burridge R, Ormandy D. (eds). E&FN Spon. London. 1993.

17 Boardman B. *Fuel Poverty and the Greenhouse Effect*. National Fuel Campaign, Neighbourhood Energy Action Heatwise. Glasgow. Friends of the Earth. 1990.

18 Smith S. *Housing and Health: A Review and Research Agenda*. Centre for Housing Research, University of Glasgow. 1989.

19   Lowry S. **Housing and Health.** British Medical Journal. London. 1991.

20   Byrne DS, Harrisson SP, Keithley J, McCarthy P. **Relationship between Housing Conditions and the Health of Council Tenants.** Gower. Aldershot. 1986.

21   Ineichen B. **Homes and Health.** E&FN Spon. London 1993.

22   Burridge R, Ormandy D. **Unhealthy Housing: Research, Remedies and Reform.** E&FN Spon. London. 1993.

23   Ranson R. **Housing and Health: A Practical Guide.** WHO and E&FN Spon. 1991.

24   Blaxter M. **Health and Life-styles.** Tavistock/Routledge. London. 1990.

25   Fogelman K, Fox J, Power C. **Class and Tenure Mobility. Do they Explain the Social Inequalities in Health among Young Adults in Britain?** National Child Development Study Working Paper No 21. Social Statistics Research Unit, City University, London. 1987.

26   Kogevinas M. **Social-demographic differences in cancer survival 1971-83.** HMSO. London. 1990.

27   Barker DJP, Coggon D, Osmond C, Wickham C. **Poor housing in childhood and high rates of stomach cancer in England and Wales.** British Journal of Cancer 1990;61:575-578.

28   McCarthy P, Byrne D, Harrisson S, Keithley J. **Respiratory conditions: effect of housing and other factors.** Journal of Epidemiology and Community Health 1985;39:15-19.

29   Strachan DP. **Damp Housing and Childhood asthma: Validation of reporting of symptoms.** British Medical Journal 1988;297:1223-6.

30   Martin CJ, Platt SD,g: Hunt SM. **Housing conditions and ill health.** British Medical Journal 1987;294:1125-1127.

31   Teale C, Cundall DB, Pearson SB. **Outbreak of tuberculosis in a poor urban community.** Journal of Infection 23, 327-9.

32   Hannay DR. **Mental Health and High Flats.** Journal of Chronic Diseases 1981;34:431-2.

33   Ineichen B. **Homes & Health.** E&FN Spon. 1993 p67.

34   Watson S. **Accommodating inequality: Gender & Housing.** Allen & Unwin. Sydney. 1988.

35   Gabe J, Williams P. **'Women, Crowding and Mental Health.'** In **Unhealthy Housing.** Burridge R, Ormandy D. (eds). E&FN Spon.London. 1993.

36   Duvall D, Booth A. **The Housing Environment and Women's Health.** Journal of Health & Social Behaviour. 1978;19:410-417.

37   Brown G W, Harris T. **Social Origins of Depression.** Tavistock. 1978.

38   Lonsdale S. The Observer. 11 April 1993 p3.

39   **Communicable disease statistics. Statistical Tables, 1991.** OPCS. HMSO. London. 1993.

40   Creedon J, Murphy G. **Economic Impact of Dysentery.** Environmental Health. June 1993, pp176-179.

41   See 39.

42   Holder P, Legg H. **Mediation in noise disputes.** Environmental Health. February 1993. pp51-54.

43   Henshaw DL, Eatough JP, Richardson RB. **Radon as a causative factor in induction of myeloid leukaemia and other cancers.** Lancet 1990;335:1008-12.

44   O'Riordan MC. **Human exposure to radon in homes: recommendations for the practical application of the Board's statement.** Chilton: National Radiological Protection Board. 1990.

45   Cliff KD. **Radon remedies in dwellings.** Radiological Protection Bulletin. 1987;79:11-4.

46   Florey CV, Melia RJ, Chinn S, et al. **The relationship between respiratory illness in primary school children and the use of gas for cooking.** International Journal of Epidemiology. 1979;8:347-53.

47   Anonymous. **Rat Scandal.** Daily Hazard. 1988;19:1.

48   Constantinides P. *Safe at home? Children's accidents and inequality.* Radical Community Medicine 1988; Spring: 31-4.

49   Lowry S. British Medical Journal 1991;303:838-40.

50   *Homeless families and their health.* Health Visitors Association and the British Medical Association. London. 1989.

51   Conway J (ed). *Prescription for poor health: the crisis for homeless families.* London Food Commission, Maternity Alliance, SHAC, Shelter. London. 1988.

52   Victor CR. *Health status of the temporarily homeless population and residents of North West Thames region.* British Medical Journal 1992;305:387-91.

53   Patterson K, Roderick PJ. *Obstetric outcome in homeless women.* British Medical Journal 1990;301:263.

54   Toon PD et al. *Audit of work at a medical centre for the homeless over one year.* Journal of the Royal College of General Practitioners. March 1987;37:120-2.

55   Drake M, et al. *Single and Homeless.* HMSO. London. 1982.

56   Scott R, Gaskell PG, Morrells DC. *Patients who reside in common lodging houses.* British Medical Journal 1966;2:1561-64.

57   Ramsden S. *'Approaches to medical care of homeless people in central London.'* In: *Housing for Health.* Smith SJ. Knill-Jones R, McGuckin A.(Eds). Longman UK. 1991.

58   Tandon PK. *Health care for the homeless.* Journal of the Royal College of General Practitioners. June 1986;36:292.

59   Marshall M. *Collected and neglected: are Oxford hostels for the homeless filling up with disabled psychiatric patients?* BMJ 1989;299:706-9.

60   Weller M, Tobiansky, Hollander D,Ibrahimi S. *Psychosis and destitution at Christmas 1985-1988.* Lancet 1989;ii:1509-1511.

61   Timms PW, Fry AH. *Homelessness and mental illness.* Health Trends, London. 1989, August Vol 21 No. 3 pp70-71.

62   James A. *Homeless women in London: the hostel perspective.* Health Trends 1991;23(2):80-83.

63   Breakey WR, Fischer PJ, Kramer M, Nestadt G, Romanoski AJ, Ross A, Royall RM, Stine OC. *Health and Mental Health Problems of Homeless Men and Women in Baltimore.* Journal of the American Medical Association. 1989;262:10:1352-1357.

64   *Fit for Nothing? Young people, benefits and Youth Training.* The Children's Society for the Coalition on Young People and Social Security. 1991.

65   *Young People and Severe Hardship.* The Coalition on Young People and Social Security. Undated.

66   Coid J. *Mentally abnormal prisoners on remand: Rejected or accepted by the NHS?* British Medical Journal 1988;296:1779-1782.

67   See 52.

68   Victor C, Connelly J, Roderick P, et al. *The use of hospital services by homeless people in an inner London health district.* British Medical Journal 1989;299:725.

69   Old P. *Homelessness and Primary Care.* Southampton. April 1993.

70   National Council For Voluntary Organisations, NCVO News. April 1993;43:9.

71   Griffiths R. *Community Care: Agenda for Action.* HMSO, 1988.

72   Clapham D, et al. *Housing and Social Policy.* Blackwell. 1990.

73   Major City Councils' Housing Group. *Housing and Community Care: A challenge to Local Authorities.* August 1988, p29.

74   *Caring for People: Community Care in the Next Decade and Beyond.* HMSO. November 1989.

75   Arnold P, Page D. *Bricks and Mortar or Foundations for Action? Housing and Community Care.* The School of Social and Professional Studies, Humberside Polytechnic, Hull. 1992. p6.

76   Hoyes L, Means R. *Implementing the White Paper on Community Care. Studies in decentralisation and quasi markets.* University of Bristol. 1991.

77   Watson L, Ward D. *Assessing Housing Needs for Community Care.* Housing and Planning Review. July 1993. p24.
78   ibid
79   *The Health of the Nation: A Strategy for Health in England.* HMSO. London. 1992.
80   Thomas A, Niner P. *Living in Temporary Accommodation: a Survey of Homeless People.* HMSO. London. 1989.

2 Social housing in crisis

1   *Public Expenditure Analysis to 1993/94. General Government Expenditure in Real Terms 1978/79 to 1992/93.* Cmnd 2219. HMSO.
2   ibid
3   O'Higgins M. *Rolling back the welfare state: the Rhetoric and Reality of Public Expenditure and Social policy under the Conservative Government* in: Jones C, Stevenson J (eds) *The Year Book of Social Policy in Britain 1982.* Routledge and Kegan Paul. 1983.
4   Malpass P, Murie A. *Housing Policy and Practice.* MacMillan, third edition. Page 92.
5   Wilcox S. *Housing Finance Review.* Joseph Rowntree Foundation 1993.
6   Roof. January/February 1991 and DOE Housing and Construction Statistics Quarterly, HMSO.
7   Department of the Environment. *English House Condition Survey: 1991. Preliminary Report on Unfit Dwellings.* London HMSO. 1993.
8   Niner P. *Housing Needs in the 1990s: An Interim Assessment.* National Housing Forum. 1990.
9   *Census Data.* Office of Population Censuses and Surveys.
10   *Household Projections: England 1989-2011.* Department of the Environment. HMSO 1991.
11   Association of District Councils and House Builders Federation. *Bridging the Affordability Gap in 1990.*
12   Whitehead C, Kleinman M. *A Review of Housing Assessment.* Housing Corporation. 1992.
13   ibid.
14   ibid.
15   Hansard, written reply, 26 May 1993, col 617.
16   Financial Times. 5th February 1993.
17   Davis, Page. *Building for Communities.* Joseph Rowntree Foundation 1993.
18   Davis, Page. *Housing for the Have Nots.* Roof, July/ August 1993.
19   See 5.
20   Department of the Environment, Scottish Office, Welsh Office, *Social Trends.*
21   Kettlewell J. *Looking for solutions to homelessness.* Public Finance and Accountancy. 1st May 1992.
22   Lambert C, Jeffers S, Burton P, Bramley G. *Homelessness in Rural Areas.* Rural Development Commission. Rural Research Series. 1992.
23   ibid
24   Morris J. *Freedom to Loose.* Shelter 1988. p 6.
25   *Poverty in Kirklees: A Statement of the Extent and Effects of Poverty on the People of Kirklees.* Kirklees Metropolitan Council. December 1992. p 15.
26   Chartered Institute of Public Finance and Accountancy. *Homelessness Statistics, 1991-92, Actuals.*
27   Burrows L, Walentowicz P. *Homes Cost Less Than Homelessness.* Shelter 1992. p 23.
28   ibid p 8.

29   *The Faces of Homelessness in London. Interim report to the Salvation Army,* University of Surrey 1989.
30   Randall G, Brown S. *The Rough Sleepers Initiative: An Evaluation.* Department of the Environment. HMSO. London. 1993.
31   Timms P. *Homelessness and Mental Illness.* Health Trends 1989;21:70-1.
32   Leff J. *All the homeless people — where do they all come from?* British Medical Journal 1993:306:669-70.
33   *Homes for the Future, Standards for New Housing Development.* 1983.
34   *A Time to Take Stock.* ADC. 1989.
35   Perry J. *Housing Renewal: The Roof Over Your Head.* Labour Housing Group. 1992.
36   Garside P. *Improving Poor Housing.* Roof, 1990.
37   ibid.
38   Inside Housing. Vol II No.24, 25 June 1993.
39   Commission for Racial Equality. *Race and Housing in Liverpool: A Research Report.* London 1984.
40   Muir Gray JA. *Housing, Health and Illness.* British Medical Journal 1978;2:100-101.
41   Prescott-Clarke P, Allen P, Morrissey C. *Queueing for Housing: a study of Council housing waiting lists.* London. HMSO. 1988.
42   Howells EL. *Medical Rehousing.* British Medical Journal 1984;288:201-202.
43   Prescott-Clarke P, Allen P, Morrissey C. See 41. 1988.
44   Parsons L. *Medical Priority for Rehousing.* Public Health 1987;101:435-41.
45   Battersby S. *Health and Housing — Observations on General Practitioners' Assessments.* Paper presented to the conference on Unhealthy Housing: A Diagnosis. University of Warwick, 1986 in Smith S. *Housing and Health: A review and research agenda.* Centre for Housing Research. 1989.
46   Centre for Housing Research. *The nature and effectiveness of housing management in England. A report to the Department of the Environment.* Glasgow: Centre for Housing Research. 1988.
47   Parsons L. See above, 1987.
48   Muir Gray JA, Yarnell WG. *Housing, Health and Illness.* Housing 1979;15:12:10-13.
49   Hodgson S. *Criteria for Rehousing on Medical Grounds.* Public Health. London 1975;90:15-20.
50   Morris J. *Our Homes, Our Rights: Housing Independent Living, and Physically Disabled People.* Shelter 1990. p 34.
51   Blackman T, Harrington B, Keenan P. *Health Gain Relieves Pain.* Housing July 1993.
52   Morris J. *Our Homes, Our Rights: Housing Independent Living, and Physically Disabled People.* Shelter 1990.
53   Audit Commission. *Managing the Crisis in Council Housing.* HMSO, 1986.
54   News and Views. Housing Review. 1993:42:1:3.
55   Department of Employment. Employment Gazette. May 1989.
56   Maclennan D, Gibb K, Moore A. *Paying for Britain's Housing.* Joseph Rowntree Foundation in Association with the National Federation of Housing Associations. November 1990.
57   Burrows L, Phelps L, Walentowicz P. *For whose benefit?* Citizens Advice Bureaux and Shelter. London. 1993.
58   Wilcox S. *Housing Finance Review 1993.* Joseph Rowntree Foundation. June 1993.
59   Ford J. *Mortgage Repossessions. Paper to the Housing Studies Association* September 1992.
60   Slaughter J. *Repossessions down but thousands still out.* The Observer, 1 August 1993, p27.
61   Ford. See 59.
62   *More Homes! — But are they affordable?* National Federation of Housing Associations, June 1992.
63   P Askew et al. *Rental Trends in England and Wales.* Housing Review, Vol 42 No 1 Jan/Feb 1993.

64   Hancock KE. *Economic Principles of 'Affordability'.* Urban Studies Vol 30 No 1
      Feb 1993.

3 Towards an equitable housing strategy

1   Burrows L, Walentowicz P. *Homes cost less than homelessness.* Shelter Publications
     1992.
2   Meen G. *"Housing and the economy — an over-reliance on interest rates?"* in
     Housing Finance Review 1993. ed Wilcox S. Joseph Rowntree Trust. 1993.
3   Aughton H, with Malpass P. *Housing Finance: A Basic Guide.* Shelter Publication
     1990.
4   Ermish J. *Housing Finance: Who Gains?* Policy Study Institute. 1984.
6   Burrows L, Phelps E, Walentowicz P. *For Whose Benefit: The Housing Benefit
     Scheme Reviewed.* Citizens Advice Bureau and Shelter. !993.